Goshen Evangel

W9-DEB-833

# MIDDLER/JUNIOR
# GREAT WORSHIP FOR KIDS

# JESUS, OUR LORD

STANDARD
PUBLISHING
Cincinnati, Ohio

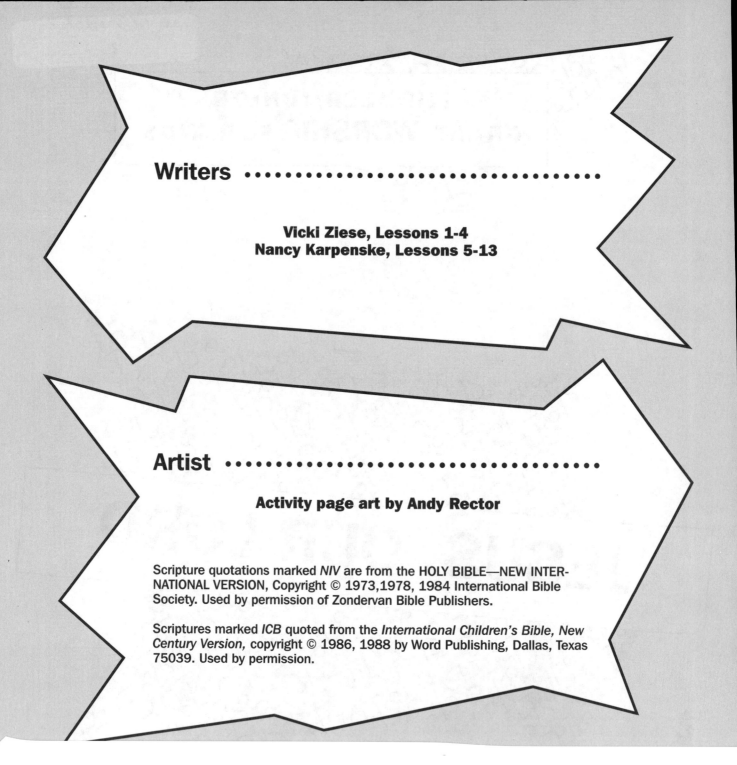

## Writers ••••••••••••••••••••••••••••••••

**Vicki Ziese, Lessons 1-4**
**Nancy Karpenske, Lessons 5-13**

## Artist ••••••••••••••••••••••••••••••••

**Activity page art by Andy Rector**

Scripture quotations marked *NIV* are from the HOLY BIBLE—NEW INTER-NATIONAL VERSION, Copyright © 1973, 1978, 1984 International Bible Society. Used by permission of Zondervan Bible Publishers.

Scriptures marked *ICB* quoted from the *International Children's Bible, New Century Version,* copyright © 1986, 1988 by Word Publishing, Dallas, Texas 75039. Used by permission.

# Table of Contents

# It Doesn't Seem Great to Me . . .

## What do you mean?

Great worship . . . Our Middler/Junior worship is hardly what you'd call great.

### Why is that?

Well, I guess everyone has a different idea of what our worship time should be. Our Bible school superintendent calls it "extended session," and wants us to have a second Sunday school hour. But Sunday school is designed for instruction. Our worship time is for worshiping God.

### That makes sense to me. What do the parents think?

Some of them want us to have a carbon

**Absolutely. And you're not just keeping them occupied while their parents are in worship, as some people believe. The children's worship is as important and meaningful as the parents'.**

Yes. I want every kid there to know God personally and to respond to Him in praise and thanksgiving. I want them to learn that worship is active, not passive. It's something they themselves do—not just the leader in front of the group.

**Sounds to me as if you're right on target. What makes your Middler/Junior worship less than great?**

It's hard to involve all the pupils sometimes. There are older kids and younger kids. Some are quick and bright, and some work more slowly and need more encouragement. Some are more comfortable in small groups than others. It's hard to appeal to all their differences.

I guess so. And even if a pupil doesn't get into the activities one week, the following week he can find something he likes. But while we're talking about the number of activities in each session, what about the number of adult leaders needed for all the small groups? There are only two of us, and we can't be everywhere!

**One solution is to use a cassette recorder. Tape record instructions for one or more of the small groups and have those groups work independently. Or photocopy the instructions for pupils to read. Ask an older or more mature pupil to serve as "chairperson" of the group to keep things moving.**

I've tried that. As a matter of fact, during the week before the session I contact pupils to be chairpersons. That way I can give them special instructions so they'll be prepared. And it's good to get to know the pupils better and make them feel special.

**Great! And then during *Building the Theme* you can circulate between groups as they need attention. You can also choose only one or two activities to prepare in small groups, and do the rest of the session as a large group. And—though it's not ideal—you can always omit parts of *Sharing in Worship* if they can't be prepared in small groups.**

I always hate to leave things out. But actually, I feel as though we get into a rut sometimes anyway, so I guess it's not so bad to drop something from time to time. We do many of the same things every week. Take music, for instance. The kids either write words for a song, sing songs, or choose songs for the group to sing. It's so predictable!

**So is adult worship. Think about what is done in most churches today—the same things, often in the same order, Sunday after Sunday. Your Middlers and Juniors may not find it objectionable to do the same things over and over—they may find security in activities that are familiar to them.**

I wish *I* felt more secure . . . about how to split up the pupils into small groups, I mean. The rowdy kids want to be in a group together, and then they end up wasting time and cutting up. And the shy kids just sit and look at each other for half their group time before they can get started working together. Any suggestions?

**As leader you can always assign groups yourself, mixing the groups as you choose. Whenever you possibly can, however, allow the pupils to volunteer for groups they're interested in. The easiest way to do this is to have sign-up sheets. Indicate on each sheet the maximum number of pupils who may sign up so you don't have nine kids working a crossword puzzle while only two prepare to act out a Bible story. You can always choose groups at random, also—having the pupils draw numbers out of a hat or count off. The key is to vary things as much as you can, but always to do what works best with your kids in your group.**

And you know, the kids I lead are . . . well, they're just great kids. I love them all.

**What was that—about the kids, I mean?**

I love them.

**No, what you said before that.**

They're great kids.

**And when they worship?**

What? Oh, I get it! Great kids—GREAT WORSHIP!

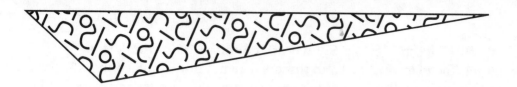

# If You've Never Used <u>Great</u> <u>Worship for Kids</u> Before,

here are some things you need to know:

This book contains 13 sessions. The sessions are based on Scriptures and lessons from Standard Publishing's Middler and Junior Sunday school curriculum.

Each worship session is planned so that pupils work in small groups to prepare the elements of the worship time (call to worship, Scripture, special music, devotion, offering, Lord's Supper, prayer, or personal praise). The elements the small groups have prepared are then incorporated into the worship time.

Each weekly session is designed to last 80-95 minutes. It begins with *Transition Time,* a flexible time between Sunday school and Middler/Junior worship. This is a casual time for relaxation and conversation. It includes a rest room and drink break, as well as a game or activity that allows the children to move around. This freedom is important after the pupils

During *Launching the Theme,* the leader introduces the theme of the session to the children. This is done through a story, object lesson, or dialogue. Involving pupils during this section is a priority. The leader also explains the small group choices and guides the pupils in choosing the groups they are interested in.

*Building the Theme* is the time when pupils work in their groups to prepare the elements of the worship time. Adult leaders work with the small groups to help them stay on track. Then during *Sharing in Worship* the large group gathers for worship time. An adult leader directs this time and integrates the small group activities so the pupils participate in worship.

*Closing Moments* is the flexible time between the end of Middler/Junior worship and the end of adult worship. This section lists a variety of activities, but each one can be dropped quickly and

# Worship Plan Sheet

Session _____                   Date _____

Unit Title_____

Session Title _____

Scripture Text_____

Worship Focus _____


## Transition Time          Leader _____

Materials: _____

_____

Preparation: _____

_____

Procedure: _____

_____

_____


## Launching the Theme      Leader _____

Materials: _____

_____

Preparation: _____

_____

Procedure: _____

_____

_____


## Building the Theme

**Group 1.**_____     Leader _____

Materials: _____

_____

Preparation: _____

_____

Procedure: _____

_____

_____

**Group 2.**_____     Leader _____

Materials: _____

_____

Preparation: _____

_____

Procedure: _____

_____

**Group 3.**_____     Leader _____

Materials: _____

_____

Preparation: _____

_____

© 1992 by The Standard Publishing Company.
Permission is granted to photocopy this page for ministry purposes only—not for resale.

Procedure: _____
_____
_____

**Group 4.** _____        Leader _____
Materials: _____
_____
Preparation: _____
_____
Procedure: _____
_____
_____

**Group 5.** _____        Leader _____
Materials: _____
_____
Preparation: _____
_____
Procedure: _____
_____
_____

**Group 6.** _____        Leader _____
Materials: _____
_____
Preparation: _____
_____
Procedure: _____
_____
_____

## Sharing in Worship                        Leader _____

_____
_____
_____
_____
_____
_____
_____
_____
_____
_____

# God Keeps His Promises

## Worship Focus

Worship God because He keeps all His promises.

## Transition Time

**(10-15 minutes)**

**Right Order.** Before the session write the names of some of the people listed in Matthew 1:2, 5, 6, and 16 on separate slips of paper. Have two slips written for each name. (Choose some of the more well-known names, such as Abraham, Isaac, Jacob, Ruth, David, Solomon, Mary, and Jesus.) Divide the pupils into two teams. Have each child draw a name from a basket. (No duplicate names should be

## Launching the Theme

**(10 minutes)**

Write promise sentences on the board, leaving a blank for the word "promise."

I _____ I won't hurt you.
I _____ never to hit you again.
I _____ to always be your friend.
I _____ I won't do it again.

**What one word could we use to fill in the blanks that would make sense in each of these sentences?** (Promise.) **Have you ever made any of these promises? Has anyone made these promises to you? What are some other promises people have made to you? What are some promises you have made to others?** (Allow response.) **Do people**

God is the only one who always does what He says He will do. Today we will worship God because He always keeps His promises. He promised to send us a Savior, and He did. He prepared a nation for many years from which the Savior would come. When the time was right, God sent us the Savior—His Son, Jesus.

Briefly explain the choices of preparation for worship. Allow the children to choose which group they would like to participate in.

# Building the Theme
● ● ● ● ● ● ● ● ● ● ● ● ● ● ●
## (20-30 minutes)

### 1. Call to Worship/Personal Praise.
Pupils will gather facts related to God's promises and write an acrostic to praise Him. Give pupils copies of activity page 1A. Have the children read the Scripture verses listed and list facts related to God's promises, such as "God's promises never fail," "God's promises have been tested," and "God is faithful to all His promises." Pupils will write an acrostic to joyfully praise God for keeping His promises. Below is an example:

Have them use their activity sheets to write a rough draft. Then provide a large sheet of poster board for pupils to copy and illustrate the acrostic. Assign various pupils a line of the acrostic to read during *Sharing in Worship*.

Focus a discussion on explaining what an acrostic is and some possible lines to use in the acrostic. Help the pupils to understand that in their acrostic they should express praise to God for keeping His promises.

### 2. Devotional. Pupils will prepare a family tree for Jesus, using the list of

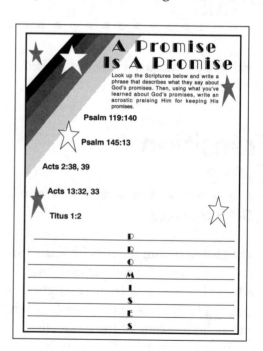

You ke **P** t Your promises to people in the Bible.

ancestors found in Matthew chapter 1. This can be done in mural form by using a long piece of paper tablecloth or freezer paper. Divide the pupils into groups of two or three. Assign each group a prominent ancestor of Jesus to draw. Before the pupils begin, prepare a large picture of a tree. The illustrations may be drawn among the branches of the tree.

Some suggested figures to use are Abraham, surrounded by stars; Jacob, sleeping with his head on a rock; Boaz and Ruth in a wheat field; David, the shepherd boy; Solomon, the wise king; Joseph the carpenter and Mary; Jesus in a manger. Be sure the members of the family tree are labeled.

Focus a discussion on Jesus' family tree. **What is a family tree?** (A way to record the names of our ancestors.) **Everyone has a family tree. Some people can trace their family back many generations. When we look in Matthew chapter 1, we can see that Jesus' ancestors can be traced back all the way to Abraham. That covers hundreds of years! God used many of Jesus' ancestors during those years who were to prepare for the coming of Jesus.**

**3. Group Singing.** Pupils will choose songs and look up Scriptures related to God's keeping His promises. Provide a concordance, several hymnals, VBS songbooks, songsheets, and chorus books. Ask pupils to name songs that talk about promises God has made to them or how God keeps His promises. Use the songbooks for ideas. Some suggestions follow:

**Does anyone know what a concordance is? A concordance is a book, or a part of a book, that helps you find places where a particular word is used. Today we want to find some verses that talk about God's promises, so we can look up "promise" in the concordance and see some verses talking about God's promises.** (Help the children get started with using a concordance.)

**What are some songs that talk about God's promises?** (Allow the children to brainstorm, then make available the songbooks for the pupils to look through for more ideas.)

**4. Scripture.** By making a folding card, pupils will write and illustrate God's promise to Abraham. For this activity you will need copies of activity page 1B for each pupil, markers, pens or pencils, and Bibles.

**God always keeps His promises. He made a special promise to Abraham. We**

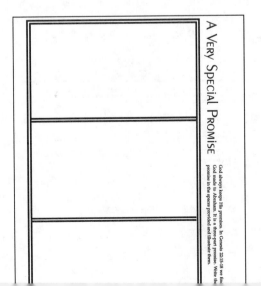

take possession of the cities of their enemies; through Abraham's offering, all nations on earth will be blessed.) **What does the third part of this promise mean?** (Allow responses.) **God was telling Abraham that through his family a Savior would be born. Who is that Savior?** (Jesus.) **From the time God made this promise to Abraham until the time when Jesus was born, God was preparing the people of Israel to be the nation into which Jesus would be born. We can thank God for keeping His promise.**

**From your activity page, make a folding card showing the three parts to God's promise to Abraham and illustrate them. We will share these during the devotional part of** *Sharing in Worship.*

**5. Scripture.** Pupils will decode phrases describing promises of God and locate the promises in the Bible. For this activity provide each pupil a copy of activity page 1C, a pen or pencil, and a Bible.

**PROMISES! PROMISES!**

God always keeps His promises. The Bible is filled with many promises God has made to us. Decode the phrases below to discover some of the promises in God's Word. Then draw a line between the phrase and where it is found in the Bible.

| A | B | C | D | E | F | G | H | I | J | K | L | M |
|---|---|---|---|---|---|---|---|---|---|---|---|---|
| N | O | P | Q | R | S | T | U | V | W | X | Y | Z |

FVAF SBETVIRA      1 Thessalonians 4:16

UBYL FCVEVG      Genesis 9:13-17

RGREANY YVSR      Romans 8:38, 39

ARIRE QRFGEBL RNEGU JVGU SYBBQ NTNVA      James 2:5

N CYNPR VF CERCNERQ SBE HF      Acts 2:39

WRFHF JVYY ERGHEA      Acts 2:39

TBQ JVYY CEBIVQR BHE ARRQF      John 14:2

ABGUVAT PNA FRCNENGR HF SEBZ TBQF YBIR      Matthew 6:33

**match the phrases with the correct references. During** *Sharing in Worship* **we will take turns reading these promises aloud.**

**6. Personal Praise and Prayer.** Pupils will make mobiles as a reminder of God's promise to send His Son. For this activity you will need hangers, yarn, scissors, tape, and old Christmas cards. Have the children cut pictures that illustrate the Christmas story from the cards. Tape each picture to a piece of yarn. Tape the other end of the yarn to the hangers. Hang the mobiles.

**Look in your Bibles at Matthew, chapter 1. This is called a genealogy. It tells us about the generations of people in Jesus' ancestry. Over the course of hundreds of years, God prepared a nation, Israel, for the birth of the Savior. Who is this Savior?** (Jesus.) **Why do you think Jesus was born when He was?** (Allow pupils to respond.) **Let's look in Galatians 4:4.** (Have a pupil read the verse aloud.) **Jesus was born when the time had fully come, or the time was right. Who knew when the time was right?** (God.) **Do you think God always knew when He would send Jesus? Why?** (Allow response.) **God knew everything from the very beginning. He knew when the right time would be to send the Savior. We celebrate our Savior's birth at Christmas time. When we look at our mobiles, we are reminded of God's love for us. We can praise God for keeping His promise and sending us His Son.**

**Call to Worship** (Group 1): **Group 1 has prepared an acrostic they are going to present to us. They have written praises to God for keeping His promises.**

**Devotional** (Groups 2 and 4): **What is a family tree?** (Have a pupil from Group 2 explain.) **Does everyone have a family tree?** (Yes.) **Some people may only know those ancestors who are still alive, and some may be able to trace their family back many generations.**

**Group 2 made a family tree for Jesus.** (Have pupils in Group 2 display their mural.) **They looked in Matthew chapter 1 and saw that Jesus' ancestors could be traced back hundreds of years. Let's see who some of Jesus' ancestors were.** (Allow pupils to point out and name people on the family tree. They may also want to tell about the illustration for each person to help the other children identify the names.) **Jesus' family tree can be traced clear back to Abraham. He appears on the list a very long time before Jesus was born. God made a special promise to Abraham about Jesus. Group 4 can tell us about that.**

Have Group 4 show their activity pages and read aloud God's promise to Abraham. **Do you know what God is saying to Abraham when He says all nations on earth will be blessed through Abraham's offspring? God is telling Abraham that through his family a Savior would be born. That Savior was Jesus. God spent hundreds of years preparing the people of Israel to be the nation into which Jesus would be born.**

**God kept His promises to Abraham. Through that nation, the world was blessed. How does the coming of Jesus bless us?** (Allow response.) **Jesus died for us so we can believe in Him and obey Him and spend eternity with Him forever in Heaven. God promises us that. God will keep His promise to us just as He did with Abraham.**

**Lord's Supper: God made a promise about Jesus to Abraham many years ago. Many years later when the time was just right, God sent Jesus into the world to save us. Let's thank God for keeping His promise to send Jesus.** Have a pupil pray before partaking in the Lord's Supper.

**Offering:** Before the worship session, appoint pupils to collect the offering. Help one pupil prepare an offering prayer. **We are thankful that God keeps His promises to us. One way we can show God how thankful we are is by giving offerings to Him. As we put our offering into the collection plate, let's think about how thankful we are to God for keeping His promises.**

**Scripture** (Group 5): **We have heard how God has made many promises to us and how He always keeps His promises. Group 5 has done an activity page to discover some of these special promises God has made to us.** Have pupils take turns reading the verses aloud from their Bibles.

**Group Singing** (Group 3): **Group 3 has found some songs that tell about God's promises. They also have looked up some verses that tell about God's promises. Let's listen to them share these verses. Then we will all sing while Group 3 leads us in songs about God's promises.**

**Personal Praise and Prayer** (Group 6): **Group 6 made mobiles to remind us how Jesus came into the world as a tiny baby. Our Bibles tell us God sent Jesus when God knew the time was right. We celebrate our Savior's birth during the Christmas season. Looking at the mobiles reminds of God's love for us. We can praise God for keeping His promise and sending us His Son. Let's pray and thank Him.**

Have pupils come together in a circle for prayer time. Allow three or four volunteers to pray aloud.

# Closing
# Moments

• • • • • • • • • • • • • •

## (10-15 minutes)

You will need paper, markers, and pens.

We've worshiped God today because He keeps His promises. One of the promises God made was to never flood the earth again to destroy it. Group 5 shared this promise with us. God sent us rainbows to remind us that He will keep this promise. Let's make a rainbow poster to remind us of some of God's promises we have learned about today. Color in the different colors of the rainbow. Then write a different promise God has made to us on each of the colors. Take this poster home and hang it in your room or on the refrigerator to remind you of God's promises every day.

# A Promise Is A Promise

Look up the Scriptures below and write a phrase that describes what they say about God's promises. Then, using what you've learned about God's promises, write an acrostic praising Him for keeping His promises.

**Psalm 119:140**

**Psalm 145:13**

**Acts 2:38, 39**

**Acts 13:32, 33**

**Titus 1:2**

P
_____

R
_____

O
_____

M
_____

I
_____

S
_____

E
_____

S
_____

© 1992 by The Standard Publishing Company.
Permission is granted to photocopy this page for ministry purposes only—not for resale.

# A Very Special Promise

God always keeps His promises. In Genesis 22:15-18 we find a special promise God made to Abraham. It is a three-part promise. Write the three parts of the promise in the spaces provided and illustrate them.

© 1992 by The Standard Publishing Company.
Permission is granted to photocopy this page for ministry purposes only—not for resale.

# PROMISES! PROMISES!

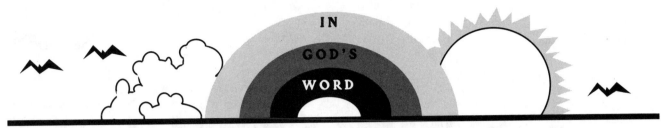

IN
GOD'S
WORD

God always keeps His promises. The Bible is filled with many promises God has made to us. Decode the phrases below to discover some of the promises in God's Word. Then draw a line between the phrase and where it is found in the Bible.

| A | B | C | D | E | F | G | H | I | J | K | L | M |
|---|---|---|---|---|---|---|---|---|---|---|---|---|
| N | O | P | Q | R | S | T | U | V | W | X | Y | Z |

FVAF SBETVIRA

UBYL FCVEVG

RGREANY YVSR

ARIRE QRFGEBL RNEGU JVGU SYBBQ NTNVA

N CYNPR VF CERCNERQ SBE HF

WRFHF JVYY ERGHEA

TBQ JVYY CEBIVQR BHE ARRQF

ABGUVAT PNA FRCNENGR HF SEBZ TBQF YBIR

1 Thessalonians 4:16

Genesis 9:13-17

Romans 8:38, 39

James 2:5

Acts 2:39

Acts 2:39

John 14:2

Matthew 6:33

© 1992 by The Standard Publishing Company.
Permission is granted to photocopy this page for ministry purposes only—not for resale.

# God Wants Each of Us

## Worship Focus

Worship God because He desires the gift of ourselves.

## Transition Time

**(10-15 minutes)**

**Gift Give and Receive**. Divide a large sheet of poster board into separate areas. These areas can be any shape or size, but use the entire poster board. Label the different areas with people the pupils probably would have either given a gift or received a gift from. (Suggestions: parent, brother or sister, grandparent, aunt, uncle, or other relative, teacher, friend.) Lay the poster board on the floor and have the pupils line up facing it. Take turns giving each pupil a coin. The pupil will throw the coin onto the poster board so that it lands on a person's name. If the coin lands "heads" up, the pupil will name a gift he has given that person. If the coin lands "tails" up, the pupil will name a gift he has received from that person.

## Launching the Theme

**(10 minutes)**

Give each pupil a slip of paper. Have them think of the best gift they have ever given to someone and write it on the slip of paper. Take turns having each pupil share what he has written on his paper. Chances are high that most pupils will name a gift that they bought.

**What do all (most) of these gifts have in common?** (Allow response.) **These gifts all cost you money—probably part or all of your allowance. Can you think of any other gifts that can be given of our time, our energy, our talents, our love, and so on. This is called giving of ourselves. These gifts are just as important as any gift you could buy with money.**

**God tells us to give ourselves to Him. When we give ourselves to Him, we are worshiping Him. Today we will learn about many ways to give ourselves to God. We can always give of ourselves, even if we don't have any money. Today we will worship God because He desires us to do so as we give of ourselves to Him.**

Briefly explain the choices of preparation for worship. You may allow the pupils to choose the group in which they would like to participate. Group 3,

Devotion, will be doing a skit that will need only three pupils (at least two girls).

# Building the Theme

• • • • • • • • • • • • • •

**(30 minutes)**

**1. Call to Worship.** Pupils will write a litany using Mary's words of praise from Luke 1:46, 47 and illustrate ways they can give of themselves. Provide Bibles, drawing paper, and crayons or markers. Read together Luke 1:46, 47 several times. "My soul praises the Lord and my spirit rejoices in God my Savior." **When God told Mary what was going to happen, that she would have a baby, she sang a song of praise to Him. She was probably a little scared about the future, but she was willing to give of herself by obeying God and allowing Him to use her to be the mother of Jesus. She praised or worshiped God because He wanted her to give of herself.**

Ask the pupils to write a litany using Mary's words of praise. Have pupils name ways they can give of themselves to God (obey parents, help people, tell others about Jesus, and so on). After they have named some ways, provide the pupils with paper and markers. Have them illustrate the ways they can give of themselves. When the pupils have finished, tape the illustrations together end-to-end to form a mural. During *Sharing in Worship,* each pupil will display his illustration and say, "I will help others (or whatever he illustrated) because God wants me to give of myself." Then another pupil will read Luke 1:46, 47. Continue showing the illustrations and reading the Scripture passage until all pupils have shared.

**2. Scripture Reading.** Pupils will discover names for Jesus and identify

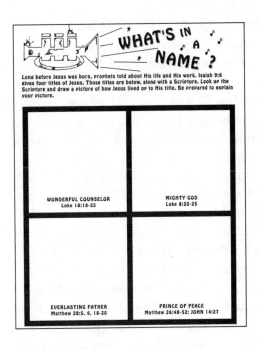

ways in which those names were appropriate. For this activity you will need copies of activity page 2A, markers or crayons, and Bibles. Ask the pupils to read Luke 1:31, 32. Then read Isaiah 9:6. **"For to us a child is born, to us a son is given, and the government will be on his shoulders. And he will be called Wonderful Counselor, Mighty God, Everlasting Father, Prince of Peace." In Luke we read that the angel told Mary to name her baby Jesus. In Isaiah we read some other names Jesus will be called. On your activity page are those four names along with Scripture verses. Look up the Scripture verse and see how the prophecy of that name was fulfilled. Use the markers and illustrate how that Scripture shows that name of Jesus being fulfilled. During *Sharing in Worship* we will take turns reading a name and displaying an illustration while someone else reads the Scripture that tells how the prophecy was fulfilled.**

Focus a discussion on helping the pupils understand the relationship between the name for Jesus and the corresponding Scripture. **What does Luke 18:18-22 tell about?** (A rich ruler who asked Jesus how to have eternal life.)

How does this passage show Jesus as a **Wonderful Counselor?** (Jesus gave the rich ruler good advice as to what he needed to do.) **What does Luke 8:22-25 tell us?** (It tells about when Jesus made a storm stop.) **How does this passage show Jesus as Mighty God?** (Only God could tell a storm to stop and have it happen.) **What does Matthew 28:5, 6, 18-20 tell us?** (The angel told the women Jesus had risen from the dead. Jesus had said He would always be with us.) **How does this passage show Jesus as the Everlasting Father?** (He rose from the dead so He is everlasting; He will never be dead again.) **What do Matthew 26:48-52 and John 14:27 tell us?** (Jesus did not fight. He came to bring peace between God and humanity.) **How does this verse show Jesus as the Prince of Peace?** (He has given us His peace and tells us not to be troubled or afraid.)

**3. Devotional.** Pupils will prepare a skit dramatizing Luke 1:26-47. Provide copies of activity page 2B, Bibles, pencils or pens, and simple costumes and props for the Bible drama. Read together Luke 1:26-28, 30-33, 38-42, 46, 47. Have a short discussion to make sure the pupils understand the text. **Who came to speak to Mary?** (The angel, Gabriel.) **How do you think Mary felt when an angel appeared and spoke to her?** (confused, troubled, afraid) **What news did the angel tell Mary?** (She would become pregnant and have a son. He should be named Jesus and would be great. His kingdom would never end.) **What was Mary's response to all of this?** (She was willing to do whatever God wanted her to do. She then went to visit Elizabeth.) **What did Elizabeth know about Mary and her unborn baby?** (Mary was blessed and the baby was blessed.) **How did Mary feel?** (She praised the Lord and her spirit rejoiced.)

Have the pupils complete the skit on activity page 2B. Help them choose parts, rehearse, and prepare costumes and props in order to perform the skit during *Sharing in Worship.*

**4. Offering.** Pupils will construct a collage showing ways they give themselves to God. For this activity you will need poster board, glue, scissors, and old magazines. Instruct the pupils to cut out pictures showing ways people can give themselves to God. Have them focus on ways they can give offerings to God other than money. (Some suggestions might be: a watch or clock to symbolize giving God their time; a child helping another, a child doing chores; a child singing or drawing, and so on.) This collage will be displayed during the offering.

Focus a discussion on helping the pupils understand they have much more to give God than money. **At offering time we usually give God an offering of money. God appreciates that. He commands us to be cheerful givers. Do you know there are many other ways we can give offerings to God? What else can we offer Him?** (Allow response.) **God wants us to give Him ourselves. How can you give yourself to God? By doing what He wants. We can give Him our talents by using them for Him, our time**

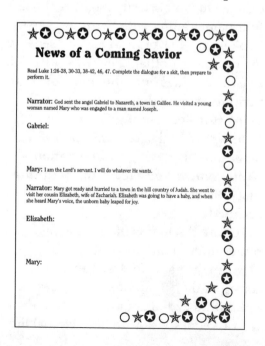

★○✪★✪ ○★✪ ○★✪ ○★✪ ○★✪
**News of a Coming Savior**

Read Luke 1:26-28, 30-33, 38-42, 46, 47. Complete the dialogue for a skit, then prepare to perform it.

**Narrator:** God sent the angel Gabriel to Nazareth, a town in Galilee. He visited a young woman named Mary who was engaged to a man named Joseph.

**Gabriel:**

**Mary:** I am the Lord's servant. I will do whatever He wants.

**Narrator:** Mary got ready and hurried to a town in the hill country of Judah. She went to visit her cousin Elizabeth, wife of Zechariah. Elizabeth was going to have a baby, and when she heard Mary's voice, the unborn baby leaped for joy.

**Elizabeth:**

**Mary:**

by helping others, and so on. He desires us to give ourselves to Him, to worship Him.

**5. Lord's Supper.** Pupils will discuss and rehearse the song, "I Gave My Life for Thee." For this activity you will need Bibles and hymnbooks or copies of the song.

Let's look up Ephesians 5:1, 2 and read it. "Be imitators of God, therefore, as dearly loved children and live a life of love, just as Christ loved us and gave himself up for us as a fragrant offering and sacrifice to God."

Who gave of himself to God? (Jesus Christ.) **How did He give of himself?** (He was a sacrifice to God.) **He gave himself up as a sacrifice for us. Let's look at the words in our song. Read through all four verses. What does this song tell us about Jesus giving of himself?** (Allow response.) **Jesus left Heaven to come to earth to suffer and die on a cross for our sake. He gave himself as a sacrifice so that you and I could be saved from our sins. Because of His sacrifice, we can spend eternity in Heaven with Him instead of spending eternity in Hell.**

The last line of each verse asks what we have given Christ. Let's look in Romans 12:1 and see what He wants us to give Him. (Read Romans 12:1 aloud.) **"Therefore, I urge you, brothers, in view of God's mercy, to offer your bodies as living sacrifices, holy and pleasing to God—which is your spiritual worship." How can we be living sacrifices? By giving ourselves to God.**

Practice singing the song. During *Sharing in Worship* the song can be presented before the Lord's Supper is served.

**6. Personal Praise.** Pupils will complete stories about children giving of themselves to God. For this activity you will need copies of activity page 2C and pens or pencils.

Have the pupils read through the open-ended stories. After they have read what is written, have them write endings to the stories. The ending should show how someone could give of himself in that situation. The stories will be read during *Sharing in Worship.*

What are some ways we can give ourselves to God? (Allow response.) **When we do what God would want us to do, we are giving ourselves to Him. Read the stories on your activity page and write an ending to the stories showing how someone could give of himself. We'll read these during *Sharing in Worship.***

# Sharing in Worship
**(20-25 minutes)**

Omit any of the following sections if you did not offer the corresponding activity.

**Call to Worship** (Group 1): **When God told Mary how He had chosen her to be the mother of Jesus, Mary sang a song of praise. She was willing to give herself to**

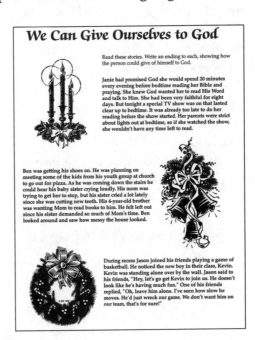

**We Can Give Ourselves to God**

Read these stories. Write an ending to each, showing how the person could give of himself to God.

Janie had promised God she would spend 20 minutes every evening before bedtime reading her Bible and praying. She knew God wanted her to read His Word and talk to Him. She had been very faithful for eight days. But tonight a special TV show was on that lasted clear up to bedtime. It was already too late to do her reading before the show started. Her parents were strict about lights out at bedtime, so if she watched the show, she wouldn't have any time left to read.

Ben was getting his shoes on. He was planning on meeting some of the kids from his youth group at church to go out for pizza. As he was coming down the stairs he could hear his baby sister crying loudly. His mom was trying to get her to stop, but his sister cried a lot lately since she was cutting new teeth. His 4-year-old brother was wanting Mom to read books to him. He felt left out since his sister demanded so much of Mom's time. Ben looked around and saw how messy the house looked.

During recess Jason joined his friends playing a game of basketball. He noticed the new boy in their class, Kevin. Kevin was standing alone over by the wall. Jason said to his friends, "Hey, let's go get Kevin to join us. He doesn't look like he's having much fun." One of his friends replied, "Oh, just leave him alone. I've seen how slow he moves. He'd wreck our game. We don't want him on our team, that's for sure!"

God and be used by Him. Group 1 has written a litany using Mary's words of praise as well as ways they can give of themselves to God. As they read their litany, they will display a mural they illustrated showing ways to give of themselves to God.

**Devotional (Group 3):** **Group 3 has prepared a skit for us to show us how Mary gave herself to God.** Have Group 3 present skit.

**What did God choose Mary to do?** (Be the mother of Jesus.) **We know from Scripture that Mary was afraid, but she was willing to do what God wanted. She gave herself to God to be used by Him how He wanted. She may have had other plans for her life, but she was willing to do what God wanted instead.**

**We can also give ourselves to God. In fact, He desires us to do so. What are some ways we can give ourselves to God?** (Allow response.) **By doing what God wants instead of what we want is how we can give ourselves to Him. What are some things God wants us to do?** (Obey parents, spend time in prayer and Bible reading, tell others about Him, be joyful, give thanks, be cheerful givers, forgive others, avoid evil, and so on.)

**When we worship God, we are also giving Him the gift of ourselves. When we sing or pray to Him, write poems or draw pictures for Him, or serve Him in other ways, we are worshiping Him. Today we are worshiping God because He wants us to give ourselves to Him.**

**Scripture (Group 2):** **We saw in the skit how God told Mary through the angel that she was to name the baby Jesus. In the book of Isaiah we can read some other names for Jesus. Group 2 has matched these names up with some corresponding Scriptures to help us**

understand these names. They have illustrated these Scriptures and will share them with us at this time.

**Lord's Supper (Group 5):** Have Group 5 present their song. **Jesus was a sacrifice for us. He gave himself to die on the cross so our sins could be forgiven. We are commanded in Romans 12:1 to be living sacrifices. We can be living sacrifices by giving ourselves to God.**

**Offering (Group 4):** **We know God appreciates our offerings of money. But He also wants us to give of ourselves to Him—our time, talents, our whole lives. He wants us to worship Him, to give Him ourselves to be used by Him. When we do what God wants, we are giving Him ourselves.**

Have Group 4 display their collage during the collection of the offering.

**Personal Praise (Group 6):** **Group 6 has written some endings to stories showing ways we can give ourselves to God.** Have members of the group read their stories.

# Closing Moments
● ● ● ● ● ● ● ● ● ● ● ● ● ● ●
**(10-15 minutes)**

Have the pupils gather in a circle. Have them toss a bean bag around while listening to music on a cassette tape. When the tape is stopped, whoever is holding the bean bag must think of a way people can give themselves to God starting with the letter "A." The next person would do the same only starting with "B," and so on. (Suggestions: "A"—attitudes, "B"—Bible reading, "C"—cheerful giving.)

# WHAT'S IN A NAME ?

Long before Jesus was born, prophets told about His life and His work. Isaiah 9:6 gives four titles of Jesus. Those titles are below, along with a Scripture. Look up the Scripture and draw a picture of how Jesus lived up to His title. Be prepared to explain your picture.

**WONDERFUL COUNSELOR**
Luke 18:18-22

**MIGHTY GOD**
Luke 8:22-25

**EVERLASTING FATHER**
Matthew 28:5, 6, 18-20

**PRINCE OF PEACE**
Matthew 26:48-52; JOHN 14:27

© 1992 by The Standard Publishing Company.
Permission is granted to photocopy this page for ministry purposes only—not for resale.

# News of a Coming Savior

Read Luke 1:26-28, 30-33, 38-42, 46, 47. Complete the dialogue for a skit, then prepare to perform it.

**Narrator:** God sent the angel Gabriel to Nazareth, a town in Galilee. He visited a young woman named Mary who was engaged to a man named Joseph.

**Gabriel:**

**Mary:** I am the Lord's servant. I will do whatever He wants.

**Narrator:** Mary got ready and hurried to a town in the hill country of Judah. She went to visit her cousin Elizabeth, wife of Zechariah. Elizabeth was going to have a baby, and when she heard Mary's voice, the unborn baby leaped for joy.

**Elizabeth:**

**Mary:**

© 1992 by The Standard Publishing Company.
Permission is granted to photocopy this page for ministry purposes only—not for resale.

# We Can Give Ourselves to God

Read these stories. Write an ending to each, showing how the person could give of himself to God.

Janie had promised God she would spend 20 minutes every evening before bedtime reading her Bible and praying. She knew God wanted her to read His Word and talk to Him. She had been very faithful for eight days. But tonight a special TV show was on that lasted clear up to bedtime. It was already too late to do her reading before the show started. Her parents were strict about lights out at bedtime, so if she watched the show, she wouldn't have any time left to read.

Ben was getting his shoes on. He was planning on meeting some of the kids from his youth group at church to go out for pizza. As he was coming down the stairs he could hear his baby sister crying loudly. His mom was trying to get her to stop, but his sister cried a lot lately since she was cutting new teeth. His 4-year-old brother was wanting Mom to read books to him. He felt left out since his sister demanded so much of Mom's time. Ben looked around and saw how messy the house looked.

During recess Jason joined his friends playing a game of basketball. He noticed the new boy in their class, Kevin. Kevin was standing alone over by the wall. Jason said to his friends, "Hey, let's go get Kevin to join us. He doesn't look like he's having much fun." One of his friends replied, "Oh, leave him alone. I've seen how slow he moves. He'd just wreck our game. We don't want him on our team, that's for sure!"

© 1992 by The Standard Publishing Company.
Permission is granted to photocopy this page for ministry purposes only—not for resale.

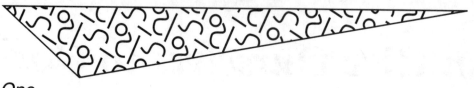

# God Gave His Son

## Worship Focus

Worship God because He gave us the gift of His Son.

## Transition Time
(10-15 minutes)

**Word Up.** Divide the group into teams of three or four pupils each. Give the teams paper and pencils. Call out a word from the story of Jesus' birth. The team that can list the most words from the story of Jesus' birth that begin with the letters in the word you called gets five points. For example, for the word "stable," pupils might list these words: shepherds, sheep, taxed, angel, afraid, baby, Bethlehem. Set a time limit for each word. Words to call include stable, angel, baby, peace.

## Launching the Theme
(5-10 minutes)

**What is the very best present you have ever received?** (Tell about your favorite present. Then allow the pupils to share their favorite presents.) **Why was that present your favorite?** (Allow pupils to respond.) **Have you ever waited a long time for something you wanted? How long? Many times, our favorite presents are things we have asked for and anticipated for a long time. When we finally receive what we asked for, it's exciting!**

God's people waited hundreds of years for God's Son to come. Finally, when the time was right, God sent His only Son into the world to be born as a baby. It was exciting! Angels sang; shepherds worshiped; shepherds told many people about the birth. Jesus was the best gift God could give to us. God didn't have to send us His Son; He sent Jesus because He loves us. We will worship God today for the gift of His Son.

## Building the Theme
(30 minutes)

**1. Special Music.** The pupils will sing new words to the chorus, "O Come, Let Us Adore Him." You will need copies of activity page 3A, Bibles, and pencils or pens. Ask the pupils to read John 3:16, Romans 8:32, and Galatians 4:4. Have

## Adore Him

*O come, let us adore Him*
*O come, let us adore Him*
*O come, let us adore Him,*
*Christ, the Lord.*

Use words and ideas from the Scriptures below to write new lyrics for this song.

**John 3:16**

**Romans 8:32**

**Galatians 4:4**

them write new lyrics for the chorus, using the words and ideas in the verses. For example, the lyric for John 3:16 could be something like this:

> God loved the world so much
> He gave His only Son,
> And we believe in Him,
> Christ the Lord.

Pupils should write the words of the new stanzas on their activity pages, then decide on an order for the stanzas. Then ask the pupils how each phrase should be sung—joyfully, prayerfully, softly. Practice singing the song with expression.

Focus a discussion on helping the pupils understand how they can worship God with music. **There are many ways we can worship God. What are some ways?** (Allow pupils to respond.) **We can worship God with our voices and minds using music. In the chorus "O Come Let Us Adore Him," who are we adoring and why? We are adoring Christ because He is the Son of God. Today we're going to use some words and ideas from other verses and write new lyrics to this chorus. Let's look up John 3:16. What does this verse tell us?** (Allow response.) **It tells us how God**

loves us enough that He gave His Son. If we believe in Him we will have eternal life. Let's put these words into a stanza. Let's look up Romans 8:32. What does this verse tell us?** (Allow response.) **It tells us that if God gave us His Son, surely He will give us all things. How about Galatians 4:4? It tells us how God sent His Son, born of a woman, when the time was right. Let's write new words to our chorus. Then we can decide on an order for the stanzas.** (Do so and practice singing the song with expression.)

**2. Devotional.** Pupils will prepare a puppet play. Borrow a puppet stage or use a table turned on its side or a large cardboard box. Provide cardboard tubes, yarn, construction paper, glue, scissors, markers, and chenille wire. Ask pupils to prepare a puppet play using Luke 2:1-20. Puppet characters will include Joseph, Mary, baby Jesus, shepherds, angels, stable animals. The pupils will make puppets using cardboard tubes for the bodies, construction paper for the clothes, chenille wire for the arms, and yarn for the hair. If the pupils have trouble organizing speaking parts, ask several pupils to read the Scripture while other pupils use the puppets to act out what is being read.

**Let's open our Bibles to Luke 2:1-20 and read it.** (Do so.) **This is probably a familiar story to you. What were Joseph and Mary doing?** (Going to register for the purpose of paying taxes.) **What happened while they were there?** (Mary gave birth to Jesus.) **What happened with the shepherds?** (They were watching their sheep at night and an angel appeared.) **What did the angel do?** (Told them to not be afraid and that the Savior had been born, and told them how they would recognize Him.) **Then what happened?** (Many angels appeared and praised God. The shepherds found Mary, Joseph, and baby Jesus.)

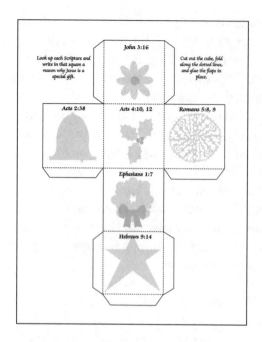

**3. Scripture.** Pupils will read Scripture verses and write descriptive phrases about Jesus. For this activity you will need copies of activity page 3B, scissors, glue, pens, and Bibles.

**We are worshiping God today because He gave us the special gift of His Son. Why is the gift of Jesus so special?** (Allow pupils to respond.) **We are going to look up some Bible verses that will tell us some reasons why Jesus is a special gift. On each side of your cube is a Scripture verse. Look it up and decide what the verse says is special about Jesus. Write it on that side of the cube. Then when all six verses have been looked up, cut the cube pattern out and glue where indicated. You can set this on your desk at home to remind you why Jesus is such a special gift to you. During** *Sharing in Worship* **we will read our verses and tell what we found about Jesus.**

The following verses and suggestions are given:

    John 3:16—eternal life

    Acts 2:38—sins forgiven

    Acts 4:10, 12—salvation

    Romans 5:8, 9—justified by His blood

    Ephesians 1:7—redemption, forgiveness of sins

    Hebrews 9:14—cleansing

**4. Lord's Supper.** Ask the pupils to read Galatians 4:4, 5; Romans 5:8 and 8:32; Acts 2:24; Philippians 2:9, 10. Have the pupils write a one- or two-sentence paraphrase of each passage, telling what God did through Jesus. Ask the pupils to illustrate the four sentences on a mural. During *Sharing in Worship*, pupils will display the mural and say the sentences.

**What does Galatians 4:4, 5 tell us?** (God sent Jesus to be born when it was the right time.) **How can we paraphrase Romans 5:8 and 8:32?** (God allowed Jesus to die for our sins.) **Acts 2:24?** (God raised Jesus from the dead.) **Philippians 2:9, 10?** (God made Jesus' name so great that we will all bow before Him.) **How are some ways these sentences could be illustrated?** (Allow pupils to respond. Some suggestions are: baby Jesus in a manger, Jesus on the cross, an empty tomb, people bowing down to Jesus.)

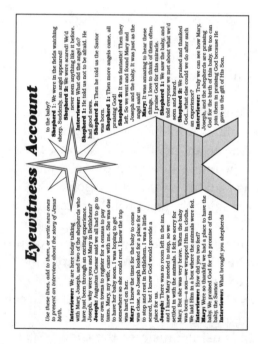

**5. Interview**. Pupils will prepare an interview focusing on the feelings of people involved in the Christmas story. The characters to be portrayed are the interviewer, Mary, Joseph, and two shepherds. For this activity you will need copies of activity page 3C, Bibles, and pencils or pens.

**28**

**Let's open our Bibles to Luke 2:1-20 and read it.** (Either read it aloud yourself or have the pupils take turns reading several verses each.) **This is not the first time you have heard the story of Jesus' birth. In fact, many of you are probably quite familiar with it. But have you ever thought about how the people who were there actually felt? What kind of emotions do you think they were feeling?** (Allow pupils to respond. Some suggestions are joy, fear, surprise, and so on.) **On your activity page is a script of an interview with Mary, Joseph, and two shepherds. This interview focuses on how these people may have felt. You may use these lines, add to them, or write new ones. We will present this interview during** *Sharing in Worship* **to help the others get an idea for how these people may have felt.** (Have the pupils choose parts and practice their lines.)

**6. Praise Book.** Pupils will make praise books. For this activity you will need construction paper and markers or crayons. Have the pupils each make a praise book to share with the others during *Sharing in Worship.*

**Today we are worshiping and praising God for the gift of His Son. What are some different ways we can praise God?** (Allow time for pupils to come up with a few ideas.) **We can praise God in many different ways such as songs, poems, pictures, writing stories, and so on. Today you will have a chance to worship God by making a praise book. In your book, you may choose the way in which you want to worship. If you would like to write a poem, use your pages for that. Or you could write a song or a story. You may choose to illustrate different things for which you can praise God. This is your book to use as you wish. During** *Sharing in Worship* **there will be time for you to share your praise books.**

# Sharing in Worship
● ● ● ● ● ● ● ● ● ● ● ● ● ●
## (20-25 minutes)

Omit any of the following sections if you did not offer the corresponding activity.

**Special Music (Group 1): Group 1 has written some new stanzas to a familiar chorus. Let's listen to them as they present their song.**

**Devotional (Group 2): Group 2 has prepared a puppet play for us about the birth of Jesus.** (Have Group 2 present the play. At the end of the play, focus a discussion similar to the one found in "Devotional" under *Building the Theme.*)

**The people in the Bible had waited hundreds of years for the coming of a Savior. God's people, the Israelites, thought this Savior would deliver them from the Romans. They thought they would be saved from the Roman government so they could be their own powerful nation of Israel. But Jesus wasn't that kind of Savior. Jesus came to save the souls of people. The kingdom He would set up was spiritual. Anyone who believed and obeyed Him would be a part of His kingdom, not just the people of Israel. That includes you and me. Thanks to God's gift of Jesus to us, we can be a part of His kingdom. We can believe in Jesus and obey Him and be part of His kingdom. We know we will spend eternity in Heaven with Him. Praise God for His gift of Jesus!**

**Interview (Group 5): We have just seen in the puppet play how the birth of Jesus took place. You are probably familiar with this event. But have you ever stopped to think about what these people must have felt like when all of this was happening? Group 5 is going to present an imaginary interview with Mary, Joseph, and two shepherds to see**

how they might have felt when all of this took place.

Scripture (Group 3): Group 3 made some cubes telling us reasons why Jesus is such a special gift to us. (Have each pupil read one verse and what he wrote.) Because of Jesus, our sins are forgiven by His blood, and we know we can spend eternity with Him.

Lord's Supper: Jesus' birth was planned. Jesus' death had a purpose. God planned for His Son to die for us. He loved us so much He allowed Jesus to die and be raised from the dead. The pupils from Group 4 made a mural showing us what God did for us.

Offering: We are thankful to God for the gift of His Son. Another way we can worship God for this gift is by giving back a gift to God. Our offerings are gifts to God to worship Him.

Praise (Group 6): There are many ways we can worship God for the gift of His Son. The pupils in Group 6 have each made a booklet praising God. Some have written poems, songs, or stories while others have drawn illustrations. Let's listen as they share their praise books with us.

Prayer: Form a prayer circle and have the pupils take turns praying aloud if they wish.

# Closing Moments
● ● ● ● ● ● ● ● ● ● ● ● ● ● ●
## (10-15 minutes)

Bible Tic-tac-toe. On a chalkboard draw four lines to form the nine tic-tac-toe squares. Divide the children into two teams. Using a Bible quiz book, alternately ask the teams to answer questions. You may prefer to ask questions pertaining to the birth of Jesus. When a team answers correctly, they may choose which square to fill. When a team gets three X's or O's in a row, either across, down, or diagonally, that team wins.

# Adore Him

O come, let us adore Him
O come, let us adore Him
O come, let us adore Him,
Christ, the Lord.

Use words and ideas from the Scriptures below to write new lyrics for this song.

## John 3:16

## Romans 8:32

## Galatians 4:4

© 1992 by The Standard Publishing Company.
Permission is granted to photocopy this page for ministry purposes only—not for resale.

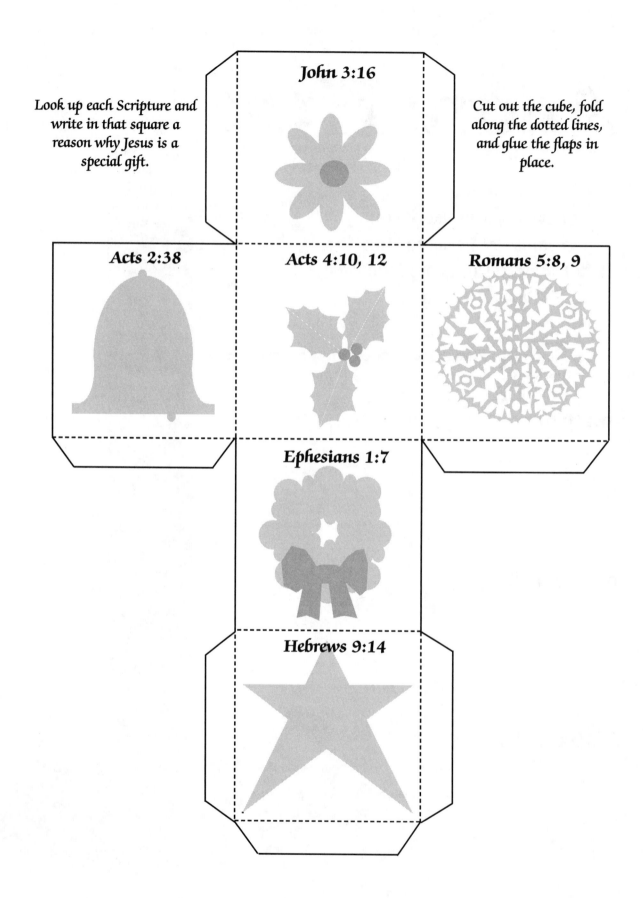

**John 3:16**

Look up each Scripture and write in that square a reason why Jesus is a special gift.

Cut out the cube, fold along the dotted lines, and glue the flaps in place.

**Acts 2:38**

**Acts 4:10, 12**

**Romans 5:8, 9**

**Ephesians 1:7**

**Hebrews 9:14**

© 1992 by The Standard Publishing Company.
Permission is granted to photocopy this page for ministry purposes only—not for resale.

# Eyewitness Account

*Use these lines, add to them, or write new ones to present an interview about the story of Jesus' birth.*

**Interviewer:** We are here today talking with Mary, Joseph, and two of the shepherds who have just been through an exciting experience. Joseph, why were you and Mary in Bethlehem?

**Joseph:** Augustus Caesar said we all had to go to our own towns to register for a census to pay taxes. Mary, my wife, came with me. She was due to have her baby soon. I was hoping to get somewhere so she could rest. I knew the trip was hard on her.

**Mary:** I knew the time for the baby to come was close, so Joseph looked for a place for us to stop and rest in Bethlehem. I was a little scared, but I knew God would provide a place for us.

**Joseph:** There was no room left in the inn, and I knew Mary needed to stop, so we settled in with the animals. I felt so sorry for Mary. But she was very brave. When the baby was born—a son—we wrapped Him in cloths. We laid Him in a box where the animals were fed.

**Interviewer:** How did you two feel?

**Mary:** We're so thankful we had a place to have the baby. We praised God for the promise of this baby, the Savior.

**Interviewer:** What brought you shepherds to the baby?

**Shepherd 1:** We were in the fields watching sheep. Suddenly, an angel appeared!

**Shepherd 2:** We were scared! We'd never seen anything like it before.

**Interviewer:** What did the angel do?

**Shepherd 1:** He told us not to be afraid. He had good news.

**Shepherd 2:** Then he told us the Savior was born.

**Shepherd 1:** Then more angels came, all praising God!

**Shepherd 2:** It was fantastic! Then they left. So we went and found Mary and Joseph and the baby. It was just as the angel said!

**Mary:** It was amazing to hear these things. I love to think of them often. I praise God for this miracle.

**Shepherd 1:** We saw the baby, and told everyone we met about what we'd seen and heard.

**Shepherd 2:** We praised and thanked God...what else could we do after such an experience?

**Interviewer:** Truly we can see how Mary, Joseph, and the shepherds are praising God for the birth of this baby. We too can join them in praising God because He gave us the gift of His Son.

© 1992 by The Standard Publishing Company.
Permission is granted to photocopy this page for ministry purposes only—not for resale.

# God Cares for Us

## Worship Focus

• • • • • • • • • • • • • • • •

Worship God because He cares for each one of us.

## Transition Time

• • • • • • • • • • • • • • •

**(10-15 minutes)**

**Seek and Find.** Before the session, write the following words or phrases on slips of paper or index cards:

> For the
> Son of
> Man came
> to seek
> and save
> what was
> lost (Luke 19:10).

Hide these seven slips of paper or index cards in various places throughout the room. Tell the pupils there are seven hidden papers with words written on them. They must find all seven papers and put them in the correct order.

## Launching the Theme

• • • • • • • • • • • • • • • • •

**(10 minutes)**

Show a section of the classified ads from your local newspaper. Probably under "Lost and Found" there are ads for lost personal items or pets. Read a few to the pupils, then ask: **Have you ever lost something? Have you ever lost something that was very special to you?** (Let pupils briefly share.) **Maybe you have lost a pet. How would you feel if your dog or cat got lost? You would probably feel sad. You would spend time looking for it. You know it needs food and water and may even be in danger. You would look carefully for it because you care for it.**

**How do you think your parents would feel if you became lost?** (Allow response.) **They would be worried and do everything possible to find you because they love you and care for you.**

**God also cares for each one of us. He knows exactly what we need and provides for us. We were "lost" and God provided a way for us to be helped because He loves us and cares for us. Today we are worshiping God because He cares for each one of us.**

Briefly explain the choices of preparation for worship. If possible, allow the children to choose the group in which they would like to participate.

# Building the Theme
• • • • • • • • • • • • • • • •
**(30 minutes)**

**1. Call to Worship.** For this activity the pupils will write skits to present during *Sharing in Worship.* They will need writing paper and pencils or pens. The skits should focus on seeing needs of others and how we can show we care for these people by helping them meet those needs. If you wish to simplify this activity, you could write some beginnings of skits ahead of time and have the pupils write the endings. Here are some suggestions: a child notices that a friend at school always wears the same two outfits; a child sees a lonely child at school; a child sees how tired his dad looks working in the yard; a child sees an elderly neighbor trying to carry out her trash; and so on.

Focus a discussion on helping the pupils to be aware of needs they can help meet. **What are some needs people might have?** (Allow response.) **Some needs are more obvious than others. We may know of a family who needs food or clothes, and we can help them by giving them some of ours. Some needs may not be quite as obvious, though. What kind of needs might those be?** (Allow response.) **Sometimes a person might need a friend or need help doing a job, or need to know Jesus. How can you help meet those needs?** (Allow response.) **As we write our skits, let's think about some needs people have and how we can help meet those needs.**

**2. Scripture.** Pupils will read and summarize Scripture verses dealing with forgiveness and salvation. For this activity you will need copies of activity page 4A, Bibles, and pens or pencils. Have the pupils look up the Scriptures listed on the activity pages and read

them. Then have them write what these verses mean in their own words. Pupils may work together in pairs. Here are suggestions for what the pupils may write:

Romans 3:23—all have sinned
James 2:10—even if you only sinned once, you are still guilty of breaking God's law
Ephesians 5:5—no one who sins can get to Heaven
Romans 6:23—the wages of sin is death
Luke 19:10—Jesus came to seek and save the lost
John 3:16, 17—God loved us and cared for us so much He sent Jesus so we could go to Heaven
Romans 8:1, 2—because of Jesus I am free from sin and death

Focus a discussion on helping the pupils understand what these verses are saying. **What do we learn about ourselves after reading the first two verses?** (Everyone is a sinner.) **Why is this a problem?** (No sinners are allowed in Heaven; all sinners pay the price of eternal death.) **What need do we all have, then?** (We all need a way to become sinless; a way we can still get to Heaven even though we

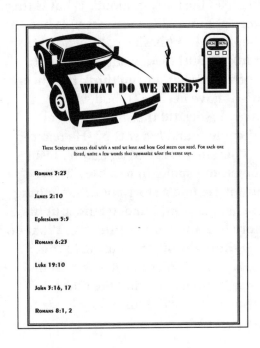

These Scripture verses deal with a need we have and how God meets our need. For each one listed, write a few words that summarize what the verse says.

Romans 3:23

James 2:10

Ephesians 5:5

Romans 6:23

Luke 19:10

John 3:16, 17

Romans 8:1, 2

are sinners.) **Who cared enough about us to meet that need? How was that need met?** (God provided Jesus.) **Through Jesus we are free from sin and death. Because of Jesus we can go to Heaven because our sins can be forgiven.**

**3. Scripture:** Pupils will read and interpret the parable of the lost sheep. For this activity you will need copies of activity page 4B, Bibles, and pencils or pens.

## Lost as a Sheep

Read Luke 15:4-7. Below are key ideas from the parable. Fill in the blanks to complete the ideas.

The shepherd in the parable represents _____ .

The sheep represents_____ .

The sheep was lost from the shepherd. I am_____ .

A sheep needs food, water, and safety. I need _____

_____

The shepherd found the sheep. God _____

_____

The shepherd rejoiced when he found the sheep. God _____

_____

Have the pupils look up Luke 15:4-7 and read the passage aloud. **What is this story about?** (Allow response.) **When the shepherd lost his sheep, how do you think he felt?** (Sad, wanted to find it, worried.) **What do you think the sheep might have needed?** (Food, water, safety.) **How did the shepherd feel when he found his sheep?** (He rejoiced.)

**This story is called a parable. Jesus sometimes spoke in parables. This means He told a story about something the people would understand, but the story had another meaning too. What do you think the other meaning to this parable was? We can get a clue from verse 7. To help us find the other meaning, we will look at key ideas from the parable.**

Help the pupils complete the activity page. Answers follow:

> shepherd—God
> sheep—me
> lost from shepherd—lost from God (I am a sinner)
> sheep needs food, water, and safety—I need a way to get into Heaven
> sheep was found—I am cleansed or forgiven by Jesus
> shepherd rejoiced—God rejoices

During *Sharing in Worship* different pupils can read the passage, define a parable, and explain the meanings of the key words.

**4. Devotional.** Pupils will make a worship banner. For this activity you will need a large piece of felt and smaller pieces of felt (to cut out letters for the banner), scissors, glue, yarn or ribbon, and glitter.

Have the pupils make a banner that reads, "God Cares for You." This can be displayed during the devotional talk and then hung in your worship area for room decoration. The pupils may need help cutting out the letters. Supply letter stencils if you have them. The pupils may decorate the banner how they wish. As they work, focus a discussion on ways God cares for them.

**5. Music.** Pupils will compose new words for the song "Amazing Grace." For this activity you will need copies of activity page 4C, pencils, poster board, and a marker.

Have the pupils read through the verse of "Amazing Grace." Discuss the meaning.

**Who was lost?** (We were.) **How were you lost?** (Allow response.) **We were lost because we were sinners and couldn't get to Heaven. By whose grace were you saved?** (God's.) **You needed a Savior. God cared so much for you He provided Jesus, so you could be saved from sin**

and death. You can now spend eternity in Heaven.

Have the pupils write words to compose another verse to the tune of "Amazing Grace." Practice singing both verses. Write the words to the new verse on poster board. During *Sharing in Worship,* distribute copies of activity page 4C as a song sheet for all pupils to use. The poster board can be displayed so the other pupils can sing along with the new verse.

## IT'S AMAZING!

*Write new words for this familiar song.*

**Amazing grace! How sweet the sound,
That saved a wretch like me!
I once was lost, but now am found,
Was blind, but now I see.**

**6. Personal Praise.** Pupils will construct mobiles showing ways they can help meet the needs of others. For this activity you will need construction paper, crayons, markers, scissors, yarn, pencils, a paper punch, and hangers.

Have pupils cut out various shapes from the construction paper. On one side of each shape they should write a way they can show they care for someone by meeting a specific need. On the other side of the shape, have them illustrate what they wrote.

Focus a discussion on helping the pupils understand how they can care for people just as God cared for them.

**Does God care for everyone?** (Allow response.) **Yes, God cares for every** single person in the whole world who has ever lived and will live. He shows us He cares for us by meeting our needs. What are some of our needs? (Allow response.) **God knows we need things like food, clothes, and friends. God also provided someone to fill a very special need. He sent us Jesus. Why do we need Jesus?** (Allow response.) **We are all sinners and have no way to get to Heaven, because no sin is allowed there. God knew we needed a Savior, someone who could make us sinless. Jesus died so we could be free from sin. Praise God for caring so much for us that He sent us Jesus.**

**God wants us to care about the needs of people too. We can show we care about them by helping meet their needs. What are some needs of others?** (Allow response.) Continue to work on the mobiles.

# Sharing in Worship

(20-25 minutes)

Omit any of the following sections if you did not offer the corresponding activity.

**Call to Worship** (Group 1): **Group 1 is going to present some skits for us to show how we can help meet the needs of others.**

**Scripture** (Group 2): **Group 2 has done some research with some Scriptures. They will share with us what they have learned.**

**Scripture** (Group 3): **Group 3 will help us understand a special parable found in Scripture. A parable is a story with two meanings. They will help us to understand both meanings of the parable.**

**Devotion** (Group 4): **Group 4 has made a banner saying "God Cares for**

You" to display in our room. Every time we look at the banner we can be thankful God cares for us. Have pupils hold up the banner during the devotional talk.

We just heard from Group 3 about the parable of the lost sheep. We learned that we are like lost sheep. What need do we have? (Allow response.) We need a way to be forgiven of our sins so we can get to Heaven. The Bible tells us how we all are sinners. And no sinners can go to Heaven. God saw our need for a Savior —someone to save us from our sins. How did God provide that need for us? He sent us His Son, Jesus. Because of Jesus, we can be made sinless. We have a way to spend eternity with Him in Heaven. God cares for us so much He provided our need through Jesus. Today we are worshiping God for caring for each one of us. The Bible tells us Heaven rejoices when one sinner comes to God.

We can also worship God by helping other people who have needs. We saw in the skits by Group 1 how there are many people with many needs. We can help meet their needs, just as God cared for us and met our greatest need.

Lord's Supper: We are thankful God cared so much for us that He sent His only Son to die for us. Because God cared for us, He provided Jesus so we could be made sinless. Now we know we can spend eternity in Heaven with Him. Let's think about these things as we take the Lord's Supper.

Offering: We know how God gave us Jesus. God also provides our other needs. We can show our thanks to God by helping meet the needs of others.

When we give our offerings, they are used to help meet needs.

Have one or two pupils take up the collection.

Music (Group 5): Have Group 5 sing "Amazing Grace" and then the verse they wrote. Distribute activity page 4C for the other pupils to use as a song sheet. Then they can all sing the new verse from the poster board.

Personal Praise (Group 6): Group 6 has made mobiles showing ways we can help meet the needs of others. God cared enough for us to send us a Savior. We can show we care for people by meeting their needs. Have the pupils tell about their mobiles.

# Closing Moments

(10-15 minutes)

You will need paper, scissors, markers, and pens.

Today we have worshiped God for caring for each one of us. He provides what we need. A very special need we had is that of a Savior, so our sins could be forgiven and we could spend eternity in Heaven with God. We will make bookmarks to keep in our Bibles to remind us how much God cares for us.

Cut out the bookmarks. On one side have the pupils write "God Cares for Me." On the other side have pupils write, "He provides _____." They may fill in the blank however they wish. Then they may decorate the bookmarks.

# WHAT DO WE NEED?

These Scripture verses deal with a need we have and how God meets our need. For each one listed, write a few words that summarize what the verse says.

**ROMANS 3:23**

**JAMES 2:10**

**EPHESIANS 5:5**

**ROMANS 6:23**

**LUKE 19:10**

**JOHN 3:16, 17**

**ROMANS 8:1, 2**

© 1992 by The Standard Publishing Company.
Permission is granted to photocopy this page for ministry purposes only—not for resale.

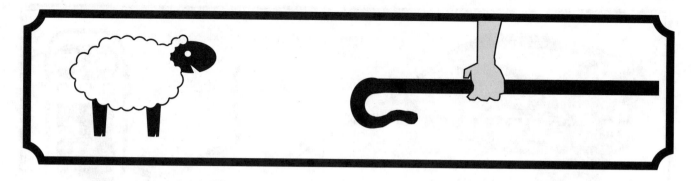

# Lost as a Sheep

*Read Luke 15:4-7. Below are key ideas from the parable. Fill in the blanks to complete the ideas.*

The shepherd in the parable represents _____.

The sheep represents _____.

The sheep was lost from the shepherd. I am _____.

A sheep needs food, water, and safety. I need _____

_____

The shepherd found the sheep. God _____

_____

The shepherd rejoiced when he found the sheep. God _____

_____

© 1992 by The Standard Publishing Company.
Permission is granted to photocopy this page for ministry purposes only—not for resale.

# IT'S AMAZING!

*Write new words for this familiar song.*

**Amazing grace! How sweet the sound,**
**That saved a wretch like me!**
**I once was lost, but now am found,**
**Was blind, but now I see.**

© 1992 by The Standard Publishing Company.
Permission is granted to photocopy this page for ministry purposes only—not for resale.

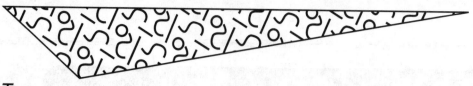

# God Protects Us

## Worship Focus

Worship God because He protects those who trust him.

## Transition Time

**(5-10 minutes)**

**Skunks and Turtles.** Before the session, cut squares of black and green construction paper. Divide into two teams: the skunks and the turtles. Tape black squares to the backs of skunks, green squares to the backs of turtles. At the starting signal, teams must try to collect the opposing team's squares. A skunk may protect himself by holding his nose using both hands. A turtle may protect himself by holding his hands together over the top of his head to form a shell. When a person is protecting himself, an opponent may not remove his square. But while a person is taking someone else's square, he cannot protect himself. The team with the most construction paper squares at the end of the time wins the game.

## Launching the Theme

**(5 minutes)**

Sometimes we make jokes about the way a skunk smells or the way a turtle disappears into its shell, but God made these animals with built-in protection from their enemies. A skunk can spray its stinky perfume to drive away its enemies. A turtle can withdraw to safety inside its hard shell.

God cares about us too. He protects us—sometimes in special ways, and always when we follow the advice in His Word. Today we will worship God, praising Him for the ways He protects the people who trust in Him.

## Building the Theme

**(30 minutes)**

**1. Call to Worship.** Pupils will solve a puzzle and prepare to read 2 Thessalonians 3:3 as a call to worship. Provide copies of activity page 5A and pencils. Have the pupils follow the instructions given on the activity page and practice reading the Scripture as a group.

**2. Devotion.** Pupils will construct a diorama of animals that protect themselves, or make a poster illustrating the protection system in the human body. Supply nature magazines with pictures of animals (*Big Backyard, National Wildlife*), scissors, lightweight cardboard, glue, construction paper, and a large cardboard box with the flaps cut off.

**We have mentioned how God created the turtle and the skunk with built-in protection. What are some other animals that can protect themselves? How has God equipped them with protection?** (Some animals have protective coloring. Some animals stay together in groups for protections. Some have protective weapons, like porcupine quills.)

Distribute the magazines. Ask pupils to cut out pictures of animals that protect themselves. Have pupils glue the pictures to the cardboard and cut around the pictures. Have them glue a small piece of cardboard to the back so the animal will stand up. Have pupils cut out grass, flowers, tress, and such from the construction paper to make a woodland scene. They should place these inside the box, then place the animals. Have each pupils prepare tell how God has created that animal to protect itself. They will share this during the devotional time of *Sharing in Worship.*

Instead of the diorama, you may choose to have pupils trace the outline of one of themselves on a large sheet of newsprint. Then they should draw the various protection systems God has built into the human body: eyelashes, eyelids, and eyebrows to protect the eye, ear wax to catch dirt in the ear canal, fingernails and toenails to protect fingertips and toes, rib cage to protect the heart, skull to protect the brain, immune system to fight off germs, blood-clotting agents to stop bleeding, adrenal gland to send adrenaline in when extra energy is needed.

**3. Devotion.** Pupils will prepare a mural illustrating times when God used angels to protect people. If you can, have a tape of Amy Grant singing "Angels," or substitute the old chorus, "Angels Watchin' Over Me." Provide a cassette player, roll of newsprint, markers, and pencils.

Begin by having pupils listen to the song, "Angels." Then have them review the Bible story mentioned in the song about Peter's escape from prison (Acts 12:4-17).

Ask pupils to recall other instances when God used an angel to protect someone in the Bible. Here are some they may suggest: Joseph, Mary, and the infant Jesus escaped from Herod, warned by an angel in a dream (Matthew 2:13-15); an angel shut the lions' mouth when Daniel was in the den of lions (Daniel 6:19-22); (fourth figure with Shadrach, Meshach, Abednego in fiery furnace (Daniel 3:19-28); and the angel sent to bring Lot out of Sodom (Genesis 19:1-13, 15-17).

Have pupils choose one of these stories to illustrate in a mural, emphasizing the role of angels in protecting God's people. Across the top of the mural, have pupils write Psalm 34:7: "The Lord saves those who fear him. His angel camps around them" (*International Children's Bible*). As they draw, have them practice explaining

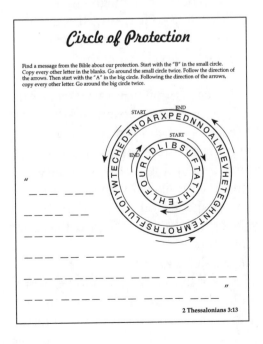

### Circle of Protection

Find a message from the Bible about our protection. Start with the "B" in the small circle. Copy every other letter in the blanks. Go around the small circle twice. Follow the direction of the arrows. Then start with the "A" in the big circle. Following the direction of the arrows, copy every other letter. Go around the big circle twice.

2 Thessalonians 3:13

the stories they have chosen, so they can tell them during the worship time.

**4. Devotion.** Pupils will identify symbols as reminders of God's protection. Have available copies of activity page 5B, Bibles, pencils or pens, poster board and markers.

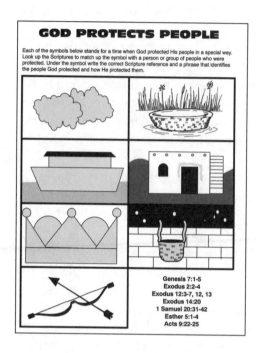

When God created animals, He gave them different kinds of protection systems. Some are protected by their coloring, some by their hard shell, some by how fast they can run. When God protects people, He uses many methods to accomplish His plan.

Distribute activity page 5B. **Each of these symbols stands for a time when God protected His people in a special way. Look up these Scripture verses to match up each symbol with a person or group of people who were protected, and with the correct Scripture.**

Cut two sheets of poster board into quarters. Have pupils draw one of the symbols from the activity page on each square with the corresponding Scripture reference. Have the pupils prepare to share in the large group time how each symbol represents a time God protected someone.

**5. Special Music/Personal Praise.** Pupils will sing "I Exalt Thee." Sing the song for the small group. (If you don't sing, ask a musician to record the song on a cassette tape.) Have the group practice the song using the words, "You protect me." Ask each pupil to look up one of the verses listed below. Have pupils read the verses aloud. Ask, **What do these verses tell us about how people feel when they know God is protecting them?** (happy, glad, joyous) **What action did the writer want to take as a result of feeling protected?**

Psalm 5:11—But let everyone who trusts you be happy. Let them sing glad songs forever. Protect those who love you. They are happy because of you.

Psalm 32:7—You are my hiding place. You protect me from my troubles. You fill me with songs of salvation.

Psalm 40:11—Lord, do not hold back your mercy from me. Let your love and truth always protect me. (See verse 3. He put a new song in my mouth. It was a song of praise to our God.)

Psalm 69:29b—I am sad and hurting. God save me and protect me. (See verse 30—I will praise God in a song. I will honor him by giving thanks.)

Proverbs 2:8—He guards those who are fair to others. He protects those who are loyal to him.

Have each pupil write a sentence praising God for His protection and describing the feelings or actions mentioned in the Bible verse. During the sharing time, lead your group in singing the song once. Then have pupils read aloud their sentences praising God's protection. Then ask everyone to join in singing the song a second time.

If you don't know "I Exalt Thee," or choose not to use it, select another song familiar to your pupils and have them write a new verse about God's protection.

**6. Scripture.** Pupils will create a poster or transparency showing how God protects us when we are tempted. Provide Bibles, pencils, copies of activity page 5C, a blank poster or transparency, and markers.

Copy the following instructions for the pupils to read independently, or read them aloud to the group:

1. Find the Bible verses, read them, and match them to the sentences printed on the activity page.
2. Create an acrostic using the sentences or phrases from the sentences. The acrostic will form the word PROTECTION.
3. Copy the acrostic on a poster or transparency so you have advice to give during worship time about how God protects us when we are tempted.
4. If you have time, draw a picture showing a person being tempted and the protection that person chooses to escape the temptation.

At the bottom of the page is an idea of how the acrostic may look.

**7. Prayer.** Have pupils prepare a prayer to use during the worship time using the Scripture verses also used in Group 4. Provide Bibles and a piece of newsprint or poster board.

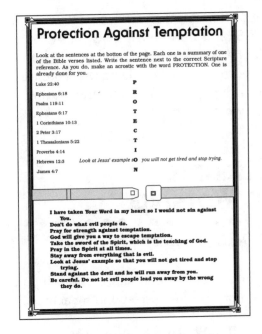

Direct pupils to suggest ideas for prayer following this form:

Praise God for who He protects—
  Proverbs 2:8
Praise God for how He protects—
  Psalm 40:11, 69:29
Praise God for what He protects us from—Psalm 32:7
Praise God for how we feel when we are protected by Him—Psalm 5:11
Praise God for allowing Jesus to be tempted like us—Hebrews 4:14-16

In addition, ask pupils to suggest simple sentences thanking God for specific kinds of protection: safety at my home,

```
                    P ray for strength
              P  R ay in the Spirit
    take God's W  O rd in your heart
                 T ake a sword of the Spirit
  God will give a way to E scape
              Be  C areful
               S  T ay away from evil
     Don't do what ev I l people do
               L  O ok at Jesus' example
             Sta  N d against the devil
```

help and protection from parents, rules in the Bible, safety on trips, health. Write out their sentences on the sheet of newsprint or poster board. Divide up the sentences so each pupil has a part to pray during the worship time.

# Sharing in Worship
• • • • • • • • • • • • • • • • • •
(30-35 minutes)

Omit any of the following sections if you did not offer the corresponding activity.

**Call to Worship** (Group 1): Have pupils read 2 Thessalonians 3:3: "But the Lord is faithful, and he will strengthen and protect you from the evil one."

**Music:** Lead the group in singing, "Awesome God" or "Greater is He."

**Devotion** (Group 2): **We laughed about the way the skunk and turtle are created with built-in protection from their enemies. These are not the only animals God gives protection. Group 2 will remind us of some others.** Group 2 presents their diorama (or poster of the protective features of the human body).

**Devotion** (Group 3): **We enjoy hearing about the ways animals are protected. But now let's turn our focus to people. Group 3 has prepared a mural. They will help us remember times in the Bible when God used angels to protect people.** If you have time, include the song "Angels," or sing "Angels Watchin' Over Me."

**Devotion** (Group 4): **God is not limited to using angels to protect us. Group 4 will show us some symbols and we will try to recall Bible people who match up with these symbols.** Group 4 presents the symbols they drew and helps explain the accounts of the people God protected.

**Lord's Supper: The broken bread and the juice are important symbols that help us remember we are protected. When we see and feel and taste these symbols, we are to remember that Jesus died as a substitute for us. His death protects us from the punishment we deserve for our sins. While you are participating in the Lord's Supper today, thank God for protecting you.**

**Special Music** (Group 5): Have group members sing "I Exalt Thee." Then have pupils read aloud their sentences praising God for the protection.

"BUT THE LORD IS FAITHFUL AND HE WILL STRENGTHEN AND PROTECT YOU FROM THE EVIL ONE."

2 Thessalonians 3:13

**Scripture** (Group 6): What kinds of protection have we mentioned so far? Protection built in to animals and humans by God, protection by angels, other events when God miraculously protected a person. Another important part of protection is the kind that God gives us from a deadly enemy, Satan, and his deadly attack, temptation. Group 6 will share the ways they learned that God protects us from temptation. Group 6 shows their poster or transparency and talks about how God helps us resist temptation.

**Prayer** (Group 7): Have pupils pray, using sentences they prepared.

# Closing Moments
## (10-15 minutes)

Lead a discussion with your pupils on how they can protect themselves every day. Review common rules of safety, such as obeying traffic laws, practicing fire prevention, stopping home accidents, not talking to strangers, and dialing 911 in an emergency. Ask, **What role does common sense play in protecting ourselves? How do you think God wants us to protect ourselves?**

# Circle of Protection

Find a message from the Bible about our protection. Start with the "B" in the small circle. Copy every other letter in the blanks. Go around the small circle twice. Follow the direction of the arrows. Then start with the "A" in the big circle. Following the direction of the arrows, copy every other letter. Go around the big circle twice.

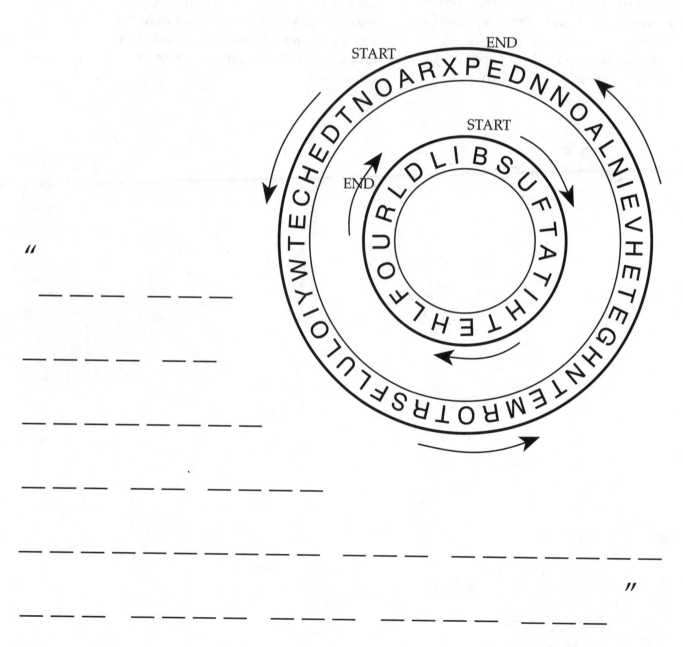

"

_ _ _ _ _ _ _ _

_ _ _ _ _ _

_ _ _ _ _ _ _ _ _

_ _ _ _ _ _ _ _ _ _ _

_ _ _ _ _ _ _ _ _ _ _ _ _ _ _ _ _ _ _ _ _ _ _ _ _ _

"

_ _ _ _ _ _ _ _ _ _ _ _ _ _ _ _ _ _ _ _

**2 Thessalonians 3:13**

© 1992 by The Standard Publishing Company.
Permission is granted to photocopy this page for ministry purposes only—not for resale.

# GOD PROTECTS PEOPLE

Each of the symbols below stands for a time when God protected His people in a special way. Look up the Scriptures to match up the symbol with a person or group of people who were protected. Under the symbol write the correct Scripture reference and a phrase that identifies the people God protected and how He protected them.

**Genesis 7:1-5**
**Exodus 2:2-4**
**Exodus 12:3-7, 12, 13**
**Exodus 14:20**
**1 Samuel 20:31-42**
**Esther 5:1-4**
**Acts 9:22-25**

© 1992 by The Standard Publishing Company.
Permission is granted to photocopy this page for ministry purposes only—not for resale.

# Protection Against Temptation

Look at the sentences at the botton of the page. Each one is a summary of one of the Bible verses listed. Write the sentence next to the correct Scripture reference. As you do, make an acrostic with the word PROTECTION. One is already done for you.

Luke 22:40                                **P**

Ephesians 6:18                        **R**

Psalm 119:11                          **O**

Ephesians 6:17                        **T**

1 Corinthians 10:13               **E**

2 Peter 3:17                          **C**

1 Thessalonians 5:22            **T**

Proverbs 4:14                      **I**

Hebrews 12:3       *Look at Jesus' example s***O** *you will not get tired and stop trying.*

James 4:7                             **N**

**I have taken Your Word in my heart so I would not sin against You.**

**Don't do what evil people do.**

**Pray for strength against temptation.**

**God will give you a way to escape temptation.**

**Take the sword of the Spirit, which is the teaching of God.**

**Pray in the Spirit at all times.**

**Stay away from everything that is evil.**

**Look at Jesus' example so that you will not get tired and stop trying.**

**Stand against the devil and he will run away from you.**

**Be careful. Do not let evil people lead you away by the wrong they do.**

© 1992 by The Standard Publishing Company.
Permission is granted to photocopy this page for ministry purposes only—not for resale.

# We Show Reverence

## Worship Focus

Worship God by showing reverence to Him.

## Transition Time

**(5-10 minutes)**

Put your snack for today on a tray in the center or the room. Arrange three or four chairs around the tray and cord them off with a long piece of yarn or string.

Tape ten pieces of construction paper (in a variety of colors) to the floor, making a path from the door of your classroom to the place where you have arranged the chairs and the snack.

Divide your group into teams of three or four. Have each team choose one person to act as their game token who will move along the "game board." Explain that the first team to get to the center will be rewarded with the snacks.

Use a spinner to move the "game tokens." As the team's tokens land on the various colors, read these consequences. Play the game as long as time permits or until a team gets their token to the snacks.

*Red:* You did not take off your shoes when you came near the burning bush. Lose a turn. (Exodus 3:5)

*Blue:* You touched the mountain where God had come down to give Moses the ten commandments. You die and are out of the game. (Exodus 19:11, 12)

*Green:* You tried to enter the tabernacle's Holy of Holies, but you are not the high priest  Go back three.

*Orange:* You tried to enter the tabernacle's Holy of Holies. You are a high priest but you forgot to first offer sacrifice for your own sins. Lose a turn.

*Yellow:* You tried to help carry the Ark of the Covenant back to the temple. You are not a Levite. You die and are out of the game.

*Purple:* You tried to transport the Ark of the Covenant back to the temple on a cart instead of carrying it on poles, as God commanded. You die and are out of the game. (1 Chronicles 13:19).

*Pink:* You try to enter the Holy of Holies in the temple. It is not the Day of Atonement, so you can't enter. Lose a turn.

## Launching the Theme

**(5-10 minutes)**

**This game was intended to show us that God's presence is an awesome thing. Old Testament people who**

wanted to be in God's presence had to follow very strict rules or risk death. Sin offends God so much that breaking the rules or barging into His presence without attempting to get rid of sin always brought destruction.

Jesus changed that. Jesus' death paid the penalty for sins. Now a Christian can come to God without fear, and without a special routine to make sure that God doesn't zap him. In fact, Christians are not separated from God at all: He sends His own Holy Spirit to live in us. He calls us temples.

So while we don't have to take off our shoes or go through special rituals to be in God's presence, we still need to treat Him with reverence and respect. Today we'll be focusing on reverence: what it is, and how and why to show it to God.

# Building the Theme
• • • • • • • • • • • • • • • •
## (20-30 minutes)

**1. Call to Worship.** This group will create an invitation to join together in worship. Provide Bibles, pencils, paper, and other materials as needed. **Little children have a song they sing to the tune of "The Farmer in the Dell." It says, "I like to go to church / I like to go to church / I like the happy songs we sing / I like to go to church." This song is actually quite biblical. Several psalm writers wrote down reasons why they liked to go to the temple. Today we will research their ideas and prepare an invitation to the rest of our group. We'll try to express some of the same attitudes that these psalm writers had about going to the temple, a place where they would be in God's presence.**

Assign each student to find at least one verse and report on 1) how the person felt and 2) why he enjoyed going to the temple: Psalm 26:8, 27:4, 65:4, 84:1, 2, 4, 10, 122:1. Then lead students in deciding how to present these as a call to worship. Here are some suggestions: They could each read a verse aloud and review the reasons given for enjoying going to the temple. They could print out a verse on the chalkboard or a sheet of newsprint and ask the other students to join them in reading aloud. They could prepare a prayer, asking God to give each student a joyful and expectant attitude as the worship time begins. They could write a new set of words to the chorus, "I Will Enter His Gates," expressing reasons for enjoying going to the temple. (Have them read Psalm 100:4 for this idea.)

Here are the assigned verses (quoted from the *International Children's Bible*), followed by reasons for enjoying going to the temple (or church):

Psalm 26:8—"Lord, I love the Temple where you live. It is where your greatness is." (Where God's greatness is)

Psalm 27:4—"I ask only one thing from the Lord. This is what I want: Let me live in the Lord's house all my life. Let me see the Lord's beauty, Let me look around in his Temple." (see the Lord's beauty)

Psalm 65:4—"Happy are the people you choose. You have them stay in your courtyards. We are filled with good things in your house, your holy Temple." (place to be filled with good things)

Psalm 84:1, 2—"Lord of heaven's armies, how lovely is your Temple! I want to be in the courtyards of the Lord's Temple. My whole being wants to be with the living God." (be with the living God)

Psalm 84:4—"Happy are the people who live at your Temple. They are always praising you." (be with others praising God)

Psalm 84:10—"One day in the courtyards of your Temple is better than a thousand days anywhere else. I would rather be a doorkeeper in the Temple of my God than live in the homes of the wicked." (one day is better than 1000 anywhere else)

Psalm 122:1—"I was happy when they said to me, 'Let's go to the Temple of the Lord.'" (a happy place)

**2. Personal Praise.** This group will prepare a definition for "showing reverence or respect." Provide a dictionary and thesaurus, blank transparencies or sheets of newsprint, markers, scratch paper, and pencils.

Have volunteers find the definitions for respect and reverence in the books you provided. Jot these on the scratch paper. Ask students to brainstorm for examples of ways that we show respect for things or people. Here are some ideas: taking care not to hurt other's private property; take off hat when flag passes or when pledging allegiance; talk quietly in library; clean up litter in a park; give seat to elderly person or lady with a child; military people salute superior officers; curtsy or bow before royalty; applaud a person's performance; treat others with politeness (good manners).

Ask each student to choose one idea to illustrate on a transparency or sheet of newsprint. Or have them prepare an acrostic of the word REVERENCE. To do this have them choose words or phrases explaining reverence, each one containing one of the letters of the word.

Here is a sample acrostic:

> hono R
> Pay homag E
> show de V otion
> admir E
> R espect
> E xalt
> mag N ify
> C herish
> lov E

**3. Scripture.** Pupils will complete activity page 6A to discover ways people in Bible times showed reverence. Provide Bibles,

pencils, and copies of the activity page. Have students locate the Scripture verses and write in the answers. If they get stuck, you may need to help them with an item or two in the code. Then discuss these questions:

> What would we "take off" today instead of our sandals?
> How would we "be silent"?
> How would we "show respect"?
> What would we do or say to worship the Lord?
> How can we honor God with our bodies?
> Would we ever actually bow down before the Lord? When or why?
> What would we wash instead of our clothes? How would we do it?
> Name a way to prepare yourself to be in God's presence.

Have students prepare a brief summary comparing ways to show reverence mentioned in the Bible with things we do today. If time permits, they could act out the actions mentioned on the worksheet (take off shoes, be silent, bow down, wash clothes) and have the large group guess.

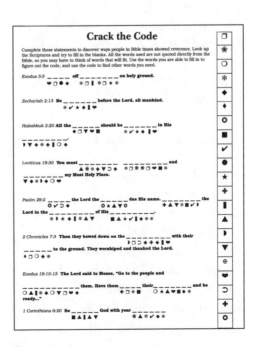

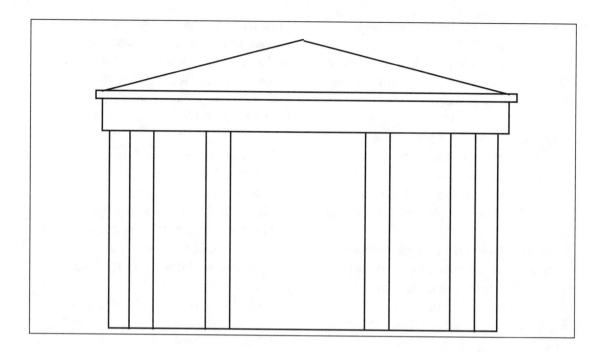

**4. Scripture.** This group will create and present a poster to illustrate the concept that God's presence is now in Christians instead of in the temple or tabernacle. They will also suggest ways to "keep the temple clean." Before the session, use the pattern below to make a "temple" for each student in the small group. Enlarge the pattern and trace it onto a half sheet of poster board. Also collect the cleaning supply items listed on activity page 6B. When pupils arrive, assign each pupil to find one verse listed below. Review the verses. Then have each student copy or summarize the verse on the poster board temple.

Here are the Scriptures to use on the temple posters:

1 Corinthians 3:16—God's Spirit lives in you
1 Corinthians 6:19—your body is a temple of the Holy Spirit
2 Corinthians 6:16—we are the temple of the living God
Ephesians 2:22—you too are being built together to become a dwelling in which God lives by His Spirit
Galatians 2:20—I no longer live, but Christ lives in me

Ephesians 3:17—Christ may dwell in your hearts through faith
Colossians 1:27—Christ in you, the hope of glory

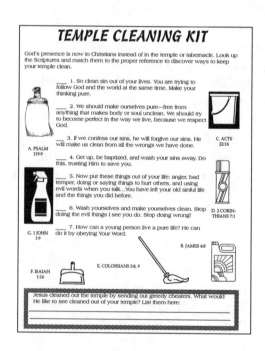

Then distribute activity page 6B. Have pupils use Bibles to match the verses with their references. Then ask, **What ideas do you find in these verses telling you how to keep your temple clean?** (pure thinking, get rid of anything

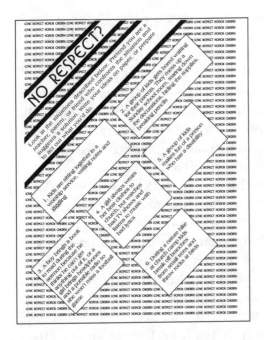

making body or soul unclean, confess sins, baptism, get rid of anger and bad temper, eliminate evil words and things that hurt others, stop doing evil, obey God's Word).

**What specific actions would you need to take to carry out these "cleaning chores?"** If you have extra time, have students create a "Cleaning List" that a Christian might use. Here is a sample list: read God's Word daily, ask forgiveness for sins, clean out evil thought once a week, start each day with only pleasant words.

**5. Devotion.** This group will create stories concerning kids who need to learn about reverence. Provide copies of activity page 6C, Bibles, scratch paper, and pencils or pens. Quickly read the six situations with your group. Select one to work on together. **How are these kids not showing reverence for God? (or, What is the problem here?)** Have pupils pretend they are the teacher/parent/friend who confronts the situation and suggests a solution. Jot down the ideas on scratch paper. Discuss this problem for only about five minutes. Then have the pupils work in pairs to create solutions for the remaining

situations. If your group especially enjoys drama, you may choose to have them act out the problem and solution during the worship time. If you want pupils to refer to Scriptures, see verses listed in other activities.

# Sharing in Worship
**(20-30 minutes)**

Omit any of the following sections if you did not offer the corresponding activity.

**Call to Worship** (Group 1): **Let's be joyful and reverent as Group 1 invites us to worship God.** Have Group 1 share the call to worship they prepared.

**Music:** Lead the large group in singing some choruses or hymns of worship, such as "I Will Enter His Gates" or "All People That on Earth Do Dwell." Use songs your pupils like to sing.

**Personal Praise** (Group 2): **Reverence or respect is not just a "religious" concept. Group 2 studied the idea and will show you what it's about.** Group 2 presents their transparencies and/or the acrostic.

**Music:** Lead the pupils in singing "Holy, Holy" or another appropriate song.

**Scripture** (Group 3): **The game we played to open our session gave us a few hints about some of the regulations God had for coming into His presence in the Old Testament. Group 3 will explain some of these for us.** Group 3 summarizes ways that people showed reverence to God in the past. Have them tell which of these actions would still be appropriate today.

**Music:** Sing "Be Still and Know" or another appropriate song.

**Lord's Supper: This special meal is one of the most important times to show**

reverence for God. Because Jesus gave His life for our sins, we can now be with God in different ways. No more taking off shoes on holy ground or offering sacrifices for our sins. No longer can only the high priest enter God's presence. Hebrews 10:19-22 says that now all of us are free to enter the Most Holy Place without fear because of Jesus' blood. This meal is a reminder that we now express our reverence to God in different ways.

**Scripture** (Group 4): **Today we don't come to church to find God's presence. Group 4 is ready to show us where God now lives.** Have Group 4 present their temples. **This group also did some research about keeping your temple clean. Here is what they came up with.** Have Group 4 display the cleaning items and read the appropriate verses. Ask them to give examples of actions for each one.

**Offering: You are a temple. God made you. He wants to live in you. He is your Master. But through all this you have freedom—freedom to choose ways to** show your love for Him. Your giving is one measure of your love for Him.

**Devotion** (Group 5): We have looked at definitions and Bible verses and examples to help us focus on reverence. Group 5 wants to help us translate all our knowledge into practical action. Listen to their situations. See if you would suggest the same solutions to the problems they tackled. Group 5 presents the situations from activity page 6C.

Today we have focused on two ways that we can show God our reverence. The first way is how we act when we come to worship Him. We act as if we are coming to a special place for a special purpose, but not because the building is holy. When Jesus lives in you by His Spirit, your body is as holy as any holy place there ever was. But our gathering together for worship is pleasing to God. Coming with a cheerful and expectant heart, taking good care of the church building, participating fully, encouraging the other worshipers—these actions all show our appreciation of God.

Part two of showing reverence for God means taking care of my own body. It's more than taking a bath and keeping my fingernails clean. It's more than eating the right foods and exercising. I show reverence for God when I refuse to let cuss words come out of my mouth, when I refuse to listen to gossip or lies, when I refuse to watch movies with violent or evil content, when I refuse to listen to music with bad lyrics.

Keeping these standards is not what makes me pure and righteous before God. Only Jesus' blood can wash away my sins. I try to live a clean life as a way of giving myself to God. When I do this, I am telling God and the world that I belong to Him. Second Timothy 2:21 says, "If anyone makes himself clean from evil things, he will be used for special purposes. He will be made holy, and the Master can use him. He will be

## Answers to code on activity page 6A

*Exodus 3:5* T A K E off S A N D A L S on holy ground.

*Zechariah 2:13* Be S I L E N T before the Lord, all mankind.

*Habakkuk 2:20* All the E A R T H should be S I L E N T in His PRESENCE.

*Leviticus 19:30* You must O B S E R V E S A B B A T H S and RESPECT my Most Holy Place.

*Psalm 29:2* G I V E the Lord the G L O R Y due His name. W O R S H I P the Lord in the S P L E N D O R of His H O L I N E S S.

*2 Chronicles 7:3* Then they bowed down on the P A V E M E N T with their FACES to the ground. They worshiped and thanked the Lord.

*Exodus 19:10-13* The Lord said to Moses, "Go to the people and C O N S E C R A T E them. Have them W A S H their C L O T H E S and be ready..."

*1 Corinthians 6:20* So H O N O R God with your B O D I E S

ready to do any good work" (*International Children's Bible*).

Will you commit yourself to showing reverence to God, both in the way you act at church and in the way you take care of and control yourself?

**Prayer:** Ask a pupil or assistant to lead in prayer.

# Closing Moments
● ● ● ● ● ● ● ● ● ● ● ● ● ● ●
**(10-15 minutes)**

**Heads or Tails Game.** Before the session, cut out two paper circles the size of a quarter. On one write REVERENCE, on the other write CONTEMPT. Tape the circles, one on each side of a quarter. Provide a dictionary for students to find the definitions for these words. Discuss the meanings of each. Then have students take turns flipping the coin. If it comes down "reverence" the student must give an example of showing reverence for God. If it comes down "contempt," the student must give an example of showing contempt for God. Have a volunteer write down the examples on scratch paper. Use the categories below if students need some direction. Students should still supply a specific action for each category. The student who comes up with the most examples is the winner if you keep score.

*Showing reverence for God:*
appreciating His creation
obeying those He appointed to care for me
joining with others to praise Him
living daily in a way that pleases Him

*Showing contempt for God:*
ignoring His commands
abusing His creation
insulting those He appointed to care for me
mocking things that are important to Him

# Crack the Code

Complete these statements to discover ways people in Bible times showed reverence. Look up the Scriptures and try to fill in the blanks. All the words used are not quoted directly from the Bible, so you may have to think of words that will fit. Use the words you are able to fill in to figure out the code, and use the code to find other words you need.

*Exodus 3:5* _ _ _ _ **off** _ _ _ _ _ _ _ _ **on holy ground.**

*Zechariah 2:13* **Be** _ _ _ _ _ _ **before the Lord, all mankind.**

*Habakkuk 2:20* **All the** _ _ _ _ _ **should be** _ _ _ _ _ _ **in His**

_ _ _ _ _ _ _ _ _ .

*Leviticus 19:30* **You must** _ _ _ _ _ _ _ _ _ _ _ _ _ _ _ _ _ **and**

_ _ _ _ _ _ _ **my Most Holy Place.**

*Psalm 29:2* _ _ _ _ _ **the Lord the** _ _ _ _ _ _ **due His name.** _ _ _ _ _ _ _ **the**

**Lord in the** _ _ _ _ _ _ _ _ **of His** _ _ _ _ _ _ _ _ .

*2 Chronicles 7:3* **Then they bowed down on the** _ _ _ _ _ _ _ _ _ **with their**

_ _ _ _ _ **to the ground. They worshiped and thanked the Lord.**

*Exodus 19:10-13* **The Lord said to Moses, "Go to the people and**

_ _ _ _ _ _ _ _ _ _ **them. Have them** _ _ _ _ **their** _ _ _ _ _ _ _ **and be**

**ready..."**

*1 Corinthians 6:20* **So** _ _ _ _ _ _ **God with your** _ _ _ _ _ _ .

© 1992 by The Standard Publishing Company.
Permission is granted to photocopy this page for ministry purposes only—not for resale.

# TEMPLE CLEANING KIT

God's presence is now in Christians instead of in the temple or tabernacle. Look up the Scriptures and match them to the proper reference to discover ways to keep your temple clean.

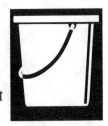

____ 1. So clean sin out of your lives. You are trying to follow God and the world at the same time. Make your thinking pure.

____ 2. We should make ourselves pure—free from anything that makes body or soul unclean. We should try to become perfect in the way we live, because we respect God.

**C. ACTS 22:16**

____ 3. If we confess our sins, he will forgive our sins. He will make us clean from all the wrongs we have done.

**A. PSALM 119:9**

____ 4. Get up, be baptized, and wash your sins away. Do this, trusting Him to save you.

____ 5. Now put these things out of your life: anger, bad temper, doing or saying things to hurt others, and using evil words when you talk...You have left your old sinful life and the things you did before.

____ 6. Wash yourselves and make yourselves clean. Stop doing the evil things I see you do. Stop doing wrong!

**D. 2 CORINTHIANS 7:1**

**G. 1 JOHN 1:9**

____ 7. How can a young person live a pure life? He can do it by obeying Your Word.

**B. JAMES 4:8**

**E. COLOSSIANS 3:8, 9**

**F. ISAIAH 1:16**

Jesus cleaned out the temple by sending out greedy cheaters. What would He like to see cleaned out of your temple? List them here:

_____

_____

© 1992 by The Standard Publishing Company.
Permission is granted to photocopy this page for ministry purposes only—not for resale.

# NO RESPECT?

Look at the situations described below. Pretend you are a teacher, parent, or friend who confronts the situation and suggests a solution. Write your ideas on paper, or prepare to act out what you'd do.

1. Kids are sitting together in a worship service, writing notes and giggling

2. A group of kids gets bored waiting for their parents. They mess up a Sunday school room, tearing down the decorations, hiding the supplies, breaking pencils

3. A boy brings a book to read during the sermon because he thinks he can't get anything out of it, or a girl brings headphones and a portable radio so she won't miss a football game

4. A girl always wears her best clothes to church, but watches bad TV shows and listens to music with bad lyrics

5. A group of kids makes fun of a person who has a disability

6. During a nature hike at church camp kids break off branches from small trees and throw rocks at birds

LOVE RESPECT HONOR CHERISH LOVE RESPECT HONOR CHERISH LOVE RESPECT HONOR CHERISH LOVE RESPECT HONOR CHERISH

© 1992 by The Standard Publishing Company.
Permission is granted to photocopy this page for ministry purposes only—not for resale.

# Changed Lives

## Worship Focus

Worship God because He changes lives.

## Transition Time

**(5-10 minutes)**

Before the session, collect props to use in these skits. **We've all seen commercials built around the before/after idea. To get us going today, we're going to perform some goofy skits about the change that takes place: Here is how I used to be; now I'm different because I changed.**

Divide into groups of 3 or 4. Assign one of these topics (if you have more time, let groups come up with their own):

I joined a weight loss program and look at me now.

I colored my hair and now I'm more popular.

I started taking vitamins and now I have lots of energy.

I bought an expensive sports car and now I have more fun.

I entered a drug program and now I'm not an addict anymore.

I took a truck driving class and now I have a great job.

Each skit should emphasize the before/after aspect: "Wow, have I ever changed!" Give groups about five minutes to plan and practice. Emphasize that the presentations should only be a minute or two in length. Each group should also write a definition for the word *change*.

If your group isn't the skit type, ask a group of teens to plan and perform one for you. Or simply have your students list the kinds of before/after commercials they have seen. Or brainstorm of list of things that people change: clothes, careers, shoes, hair style or color, habits, diapers, earrings, classes.

## Launching the Theme

**(5-10 minutes)**

Have groups present their skits. Have a volunteer write on the chalkboard definitions for change that each group gives. (to become or make different, transform).

**Today we'll be examining the idea of change. Some things in life we can change and some changes only God can make. The changes God makes are not ones we could do for ourselves. The changes we can control are ones God gives us the power to change. I don't have to change in order for God to love me. It is exactly because He does love me**

that He wants to change me. And because He does love me, I want to change, not so He'll love me more, but so I can show Him how grateful I am for His love. Let's see what change is all about.

# Building the Theme
• • • • • • • • • • • • • • •
(20-30 minutes)

**1. Call to Worship.** This group will match Bible verses showing before/after contrasts and make illustrations to highlight the theme. Provide copies of activity page 7A, Bibles, half sheets of poster board, and markers or crayons. Allow about 12 minutes for pupils to look up and match the Bible verses on the activity page. Then review answers. **What kind of change does this verse tell about?**

Distribute the pieces of poster board. Invite pupils to choose a verse to illustrate. Suggest they divide the poster in half, either vertically, horizontally, or diagonally. Then use contrasting colors, light and dark, to highlight the idea of the verse. Choose symbols or pictures to contrast the before and after concept: seed and flower; caterpillar and butterfly; tadpole and frog; fat and thin; baby and grown-up; a hole dug for a foundation and a completed house. Include a summary of the verse in the picture, or jot it on the back so pupil can refer to the verse when showing the poster during *Sharing in Worship*.

**2. Scripture.** This group will review the lives of Bible people whose behavior changed when they chose to follow God. Use the information on Bible characters below to prepare a game.

**Matching.** Before the session copy each sentence about the Bible characters, including the Bible reference, on a separate slip of paper—you'll need 36 3" x 5" cards or strips of paper. Then write the name of the Bible characters cross the chalkboard or across a sheet of newsprint. Have pupils choose a card and try to identify the Bible character. If they cannot, have them look up the Scripture reference. Then have them tape the card in the correct column.

**Go Fish!** (This game will be easier and take less time.) Before the session, copy each sentence about the Bible characters, including the character's name, on a separate slip of paper or 3" x 5" card. Deal four cards to each player. Place the remaining cards in the center. The object of the game is to collect four cards that refer to the same person. To take a turn, the person asks another player for a card needed to make a match. If the player doesn't have one, the person taking the turn may draw a card from the pile. If the person gets what he asks for, or draws it, he may take another turn. When a player collects a set of four, he wins.

Following the game, focus on each Bible character. Arrange the descriptions of the person in two sections: before and after being changed by God. Have pupils prepare to review each person's life

**BEFORE AND AFTER**

These verses tell about changes that happen to a person who becomes a Christian. Use your Bible to match the phrases below.

| # | Verse | Letter | Phrase |
|---|-------|--------|--------|
| 1. | Romans 6:23 — When someone sins, he earns what sin pays—death. | a. | I will give you an obedient heart of flesh and put my Spirit inside you. |
| 2. | Romans 8:6 — If a person's thinking is controlled by his sinful self, then there is death | b. | it is Christ living in me. |
| 3. | 2 Corinthians 5:17 — The old things have gone | c. | but what we cannot see will last forever |
| 4. | Galatians 2:20 — I do not live anymore | d. | but God gives us a free gift—life forever in Jesus Christ our Lord |
| 5. | Ephesians 2:19 — So now you non-Jews are not visitors or strangers | e. | but you were taught to be made new in your hearts. You were taught to become a new person |
| 6. | Romans 12:2 — Do not change yourselves to be like the people of this world | f. | but be changed on the inside by a new way of thinking |
| 7. | Ezekiel 36:26, 27 — I will take out the stubborn heart like stone from your bodies | g. | but our spirit inside is made new every day |
| 8. | Ephesians 4:22-24 — That old self becomes worse and worse because people are fooled by the evil things they want to do. | h. | but if his thinking is controlled by the Holy Spirit, then there is life and peace |
| 9. | 2 Corinthians 4:16 — Our physical body is becoming older and weaker | i. | now you are citizens together with God's holy people. You belong to His family |
| 10. | 2 Corinthians 4:18 — What we see will last only a short time | j. | if anyone belongs to Jesus, then he is made new . . . everything is made new |

during the large group time, emphasizing the change in character and action that happened when the person allowed God to change him.

*Peter*
hacked off a man's ear trying to defend Jesus (John 18:10)
declared that Jesus would never wash his feet (John 13:8)
Jesus said to him, "Get behind me, Satan!" (Matthew 16:23)
swore he didn't know Jesus (John 18:25)
preached the first sermon about the good news of Jesus. (Acts 2)
said, "We must obey God rather than men" (Acts 5:29)

*Paul*
followed the law to the letter (Philippians 3:5)
approved and witnessed Stephen's stoning (Acts 8:1)
"breathed threats and murder" against Christians (Acts 9:1)
started many churches in Asia and Europe (Acts 13—28)
wrote famous letters from prison, encouraging Christians (Ephesians 3:1)
said, "If anyone is in Christ, he is a new creature" (2 Corinthians 5:17)

*John*
called one of the "Sons of Thunder" (Mark 3:17)
suggested Jesus call down fire on a town (Luke 9:54)
wanted one of the places of honor next to Jesus (Mark 10:37)
called the apostle of love (1 John 4:7, 8)
called the beloved disciple (John 13:23)
Jesus asked him to care for his mother (John 19:26)

*Zaccheus*
rich, greedy man (Luke 19:2)
too small to see Jesus through the crowd (Luke 19:3)
chief tax collector of Jericho (Luke 19:2)
gave half his goods to the poor of his town (Luke 19:8)
said, "If I have cheated anyone, I will pay back four times as much" (Luke 19:8)
Jesus invited himself to this man's home (Luke 19:5)

*Abraham*
left his home and family at God's call (Genesis 12:1)
changed his name (Genesis 17:5)
gave the best land to Lot (Genesis 13:8)
twice lied to a king, saying his wife was his sister, in order to save his life (Genesis 12:13, 20:5)
trusted God enough to offer his son as a sacrifice (Genesis 22:12)
called a "friend of God" (James 2:23)

*Thomas*
called the Doubter. Jesus said to him, "Stop doubting and believe" (John 20:27)
his nickname—Didymus—means twin (John 11:16)
promised to follow Jesus to die with Him (John 11:16)
absent when Jesus appeared in the upper room (John 20:24)
refused to believe unless he touched Jesus' wounds (John 20:25)
worshiped Jesus, saying, "My Lord and my God!" (John 20:28)

**3. Offering.** Pupils will complete the puzzle on activity page 7B and prepare a picture highlighting aspects of a "changed" person. Provide copies of the activity page, Bibles, pens or pencils, markers, and a large sheet of newsprint.

Have pupils complete the puzzle. After you review the answers, have each pupil find one or more of the Scripture verses listed. On the back of the activity page, tell pupils to draw a figure showing the part of the body changed according to this Bible verse. After pupils have

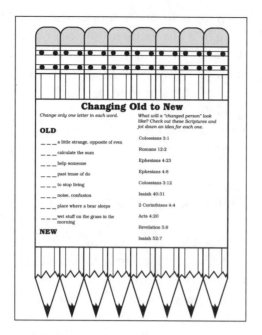

Have pupils find the verses and state the bad attitude.

Psalm 53:1—pride
Proverbs 12:15—arrogance
Proverbs 15:25—pride
Proverbs 15:27—greed
Proverbs 18:2—lack of self-control
Proverbs 19:19—anger
Proverbs 28:13—pride

Distribute the strips of paper. Have pupils write one fear or bad attitude on each strip. Then have them connect the strips into a chain.

Have volunteers read aloud some of these verses about God's power.

Philippians 4:13
Ephesians 1:19, 20
Ephesians 3:20
2 Corinthians 12:9
Matthew 19:26
2 Peter 1:3.

Have pupils select one or two verses to read aloud during *Sharing in Worship.* Have one volunteer wear the chains. Another volunteer will read the verses about God's power.

**5. Lord's Supper.** Pupils will use a box with a false bottom as an illustration of how God forgives sin. Bring a box for which you have prepared a false bottom by cutting a heavy piece of cardboard slightly smaller than the box. Explain to the pupils that they will use this box to demonstrate ways that the Bible pictures God getting rid of our sins. Have them use their Bibles to find the verses below. Have a volunteer read each verse aloud. **What happens to sin in this verse?** Have pupils jot down word pictures from each verse. Then assign pupils to draw a simple picture of one of the ideas and copy a phrase from the verse. Then glue or tape the pictures to the sides of the box. (Make sure you're able to open and close the box.)

completed that part, provide them with a large sheet of newsprint. Have them draw a single large figure and combine all the items discovered in the Scriptures.

Colossians 3:1—risen with Christ
Romans 12:2—renewed mind (new way of thinking)
Ephesians 4:23—new heart
Ephesians 4:8—full of light
Colossians 3:12—and patience
Isaiah 40:31—wings like eagles
2 Corinthians 4:4—eyes not blind
Acts 4:20—bold tongue to witness
Revelation 5:9—new song
Isaiah 52:7—lovely feet (preaching good news)

**4. Devotion.** This group will make a paper chain listing sins, problems, and attitudes that keep us from changing. Before the session, cut construction paper into strips. Provide markers and glue. Brainstorm with pupils: **What are some fears we have that might keep us from changing?** (fear of failure, ridicule, the unknown) **What are reasons some people find it hard to change?** (tradition, comfortable with the way things are.) **Let's look at a few Scriptures to remind us of attitudes that can cause problems.**

Then have the pupils cut some paper into strips. During *Sharing in Worship* each person should write a word or phrase about a sin that troubles him, either one he still feels guilty about or one that repeats constantly in his life. Prepare enough strips for the entire large group.

Help the pupils close the box and practice turning it over and opening it again to prepare for the object lesson. Have someone find 1 John 1:9 and practice reciting it together.

Here are verses for the small group to use:

Micah 7:19—You will throw away all our sins into the deepest seas

Psalm 85:2—You forgave the guilt of the people. You covered all their sins.

Jeremiah 31:34—I will forgive them for the wicked things they did. I will not remember their sins anymore.

Psalm 51:7—Take away my sin, and I will be clean. Wash me, and I will be whiter than snow.

Zechariah 3:4—Look, I have taken away your sin. And I am giving you new clothes.

Isaiah 44:22—I have swept away your sins like a big cloud. I have removed your sins like a cloud that disappears into the air. Come back to me because I saved you.

**6. Personal Praise.** This group will write a diamante (a seven-line, diamond shaped poem) describing change. You'll need copies of activity page 7C, pencils, Bibles, blank transparencies or newsprint, and markers.

Before you distribute the activity pages, have pupils brainstorm lists of words about change. **We've seen skits about change. Let's dig a little deeper into the actions and feelings about change. How do you feel when you want to change something about yourself? What are some actions you** take when you are trying to change? **What are some feelings you have when you see good changes taking place in your life?** Discuss, then hand out the activity pages showing the formula for the diamante. Have pupils begin to choose words for each part. You may want them to work in pairs or groups of three. In addition, you may want to make extra copies of activity page 7A with Bible verses about before and after. Pupils could use these verses as springboards for their poems. Have pupils share their poems.

# Sharing in Worship

**(20-30 minutes)**

**Call to Worship** (Group 1): Members of Group 1 will display their posters and read or summarize the Bible verses emphasizing before and after.

**Music**: Lead the group in singing songs you are familiar with. Suggestions are "Into My Heart" and "He Put a New Song in My Heart."

**Scripture** (Group 2): **Now let's review**

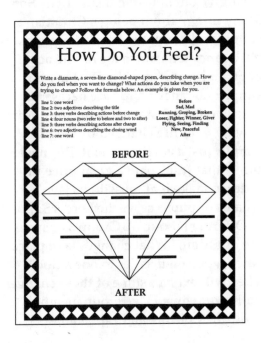

65

what we know about some Bible characters and how their lives were changed. Group 2 members will summarize the before/after events in the lives of the Bible characters from their game.

**Music.** Sing "Since Jesus Came Into My Heart" or another song.

**Lord's Supper** (Group 5): Have the small group show their box and explain the pictures of ways that God deals with our sins. Then have them distribute slips of paper and pencils to the rest of the pupils. Ask each one to write down a sin or attitude that troubles her: either one she feels guilt for, or one that she repeats regularly. Have pupils fold their slips of paper and place them in the top of the box as it is passed around by member of Group 5. Then have pupils close the box, turn it upside down, and shake it. Ask a member of Group 5 to read aloud 1 John 1:19. Then open the new "top" of the box. The false bottom will have slid down and covered the slips of paper. The box will appear empty. Ask pupils to recite together, "He is faithful and just and will forgive our sins."

Sing "Gone, Gone, Gone (Yes, My Sins Are Gone)." Then read Hebrews 9:22: "Without the shedding of blood there is no forgiveness." **It cost God a great price to forgive our sin—the dead of His Son, Many things about being a Christian are simple and plain: the Lord's Supper is not a fancy ten-course meal. The act of baptism is short and simple. Prayer is simple: no fancy words are necessary when you say just what is on your heart. Having your life changed by God is simple: just ask Him to do it. But never forget that Jesus paid a great price in order to make it all possible.** Have assistants or pupils serve the Lord's Supper.

**Offering** (Group 3): **Group 3 answered the question, "What changes take place when a person decides to obey God?" They will explain some of these changes with a drawing.** Have group members show their picture and explain the Scriptures they read. **One visible indication of change is a person's life in the way he spends time, talents, and money. People who let God change their lives often find their priorities shifting. Material possessions may not be as important as they were before. As we give our offering today, let's be thinking of how God is working even now to change us.**

**Devotion** (Group 4): **When God takes control of our lives, we are changed people, and we continue to change as we grow in Him. There are some hindrances to our change, as Group 4 discovered. They will share with us what they learned.** Group 4 will show their "person in chains" and read Bible verses about God's power.

Lead into the next part of the devotional by saying, **It is God's power, not our own, that is great enough to change us.**

Purchase flash paper from a magician's supply or theatrical shop, or use a piece of regular paper and matches or a lighter. Display the piece of paper. **Let's pretend that this piece of paper is a lie I have told. I might try to forget about the lie and hope it will go away.** (Crumple up the paper and throw it in a trash can.) **But the lie is still there, no matter how I try to ignore it.** (Take the paper out of trash can.) **I might try to hide the fact that I lied and pretend it never happened.** (Hide paper behind you or under a chair.) **But hiding the sin doesn't get rid of it.**

**In fact, there is no way that we can get rid of that sin. Only God can bring about that change.** (Light paper. It will disappear in a flash, leaving no ashes. If you use regular paper, burn just and edge of the paper, showing how the flame consumes the paper.)

**When God takes control of our lives, some of the changes are dramatic and permanent. Our old self dies. Our sins are gone. New life is born. Other changes come more gradually and**

slowly. Let's list others that we can think of, both the instant and the gradual.

    sins forgiven
    Holy Spirit comes to live
    conquer bad habits
    new heart
    become a mature Christian
    die to sin
    changes in behavior:
        temper, control of language
    discipline to study daily

**Sometimes we get confused. We look at the gradual changes in our lives and wonder why they are taking so long. Perhaps they might cause us to wonder whether or not the instant changes (which are mostly invisible) ever took place. But God is faithful. His Word is true. What He promises He delivers. If** your pupils are familiar with the song, "He Began a Good Work in You," lead them in singing it.

**Personal Praise** (Group 6): **Group 6 pooled their creative resources to write some poems that will remind us of the change process. As they show these,** consider where you are in the change process. Pray silently, thanking God for the changes even more.

# Closing Moments
● ● ● ● ● ● ● ● ● ● ● ● ● ● ●
**(10-15 minutes)**

Play "How I'm Different." Have pupils brainstorm ways that they are different from how they used to be. This can be any kind of difference. Have them work as individuals or teams. The longest list wins. Here are some examples of items pupils could list:

    Used to ride a bike with training
        wheels
    Used to be in Mrs. Roberts' class
    Used to hate broccoli
    Used to wear diapers
    Used to be afraid of thunder
    Used to sleep with a teddy bear
    Used to lie to my parents
    Used to need help tying my shoes

# BEFORE AND AFTER

These verses tell about changes that happen to a person who becomes a Christian. Use your Bible to match the phrases below.

| | |
|---|---|
| 1. Romans 6:23<br>When someone sins, he earns what sin pays—death. | a. I will give you an obedient heart of flesh and put my Spirit inside you. |
| 2. Romans 8:6<br>If a person's thinking is controlled by his sinful self, then there is death | b. it is Christ living in me. |
| 3. 2 Corinthians 5:17<br>The old things have gone | c. but what we cannot see will last forever |
| 4. Galatians 2:20<br>I do not live anymore | d. but God gives us a free gift—life forever in Jesus Christ our Lord |
| 5. Ephesians 2:19<br>So now you non-Jews are not visitors or strangers | e. but you were taught to be made new in your hearts. You were taught to become a new person |
| 6. Romans 12:2<br>Do not change yourselves to be like the people of this world | f. but be changed on the inside by a new way of thinking |
| 7. Ezekiel 36:26, 27<br>I will take out the stubborn heart like stone from your bodies | g. but our spirit inside is made new every day |
| 8. Ephesians 4:22-24<br>That old self becomes worse and worse because people are fooled by the evil things they want to do. | h. but if his thinking is controlled by the Holy Spirit, then there is life and peace |
| 9. 2 Corinthians 4:16<br>Our physical body is becoming older and weaker | i. now you are citizens together with God's holy people. You belong to His family |
| 10. 2 Corinthians 4:18<br>What we see will last only a short time | j. if anyone belongs to Jesus, then he is made new . . . everything is made new |

© 1992 by The Standard Publishing Company.
Permission is granted to photocopy this page for ministry purposes only—not for resale.

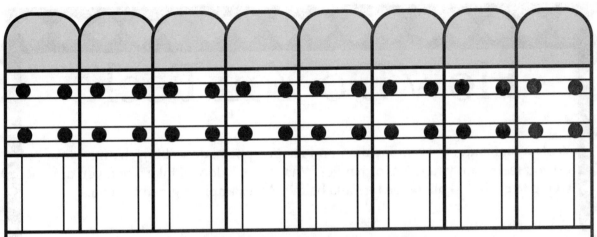

# Changing Old to New

*Change only one letter in each word.*

## OLD

_ _ _ a little strange, opposite of even

_ _ _ calculate the sum

_ _ _ help someone

_ _ _ past tense of do

_ _ _ to stop living

_ _ _ noise, confusion

_ _ _ place where a bear sleeps

_ _ _ wet stuff on the grass in the morning

## NEW

*What will a "changed person" look like? Check out these Scriptures and jot down an idea for each one.*

Colossians 3:1

Romans 12:2

Ephesians 4:23

Ephesians 4:8

Colossians 3:12

Isaiah 40:31

2 Corinthians 4:4

Acts 4:20

Revelation 5:9

Isaiah 52:7

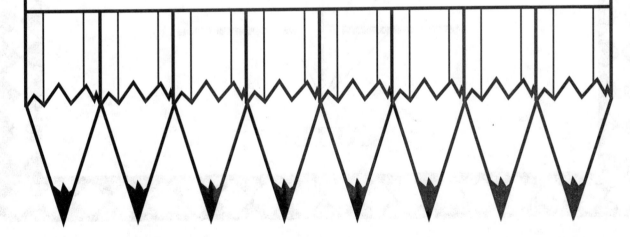

© 1992 by The Standard Publishing Company.
Permission is granted to photocopy this page for ministry purposes only—not for resale.

# How Do You Feel?

Write a diamante, a seven-line diamond-shaped poem, describing change. How do you feel when you want to change? What actions do you take when you are trying to change? Follow the formula below. An example is given for you.

line 1: one word
line 2: two adjectives describing the title
line 3: three verbs describing actions before change
line 4: four nouns (two refer to before and two to after)
line 5: three verbs describing actions after change
line 6: two adjectives describing the closing word
line 7: one word

**Before**
**Sad, Mad**
**Running, Groping, Broken**
**Loser, Fighter, Winner, Giver**
**Flying, Seeing, Finding**
**New, Peaceful**
**After**

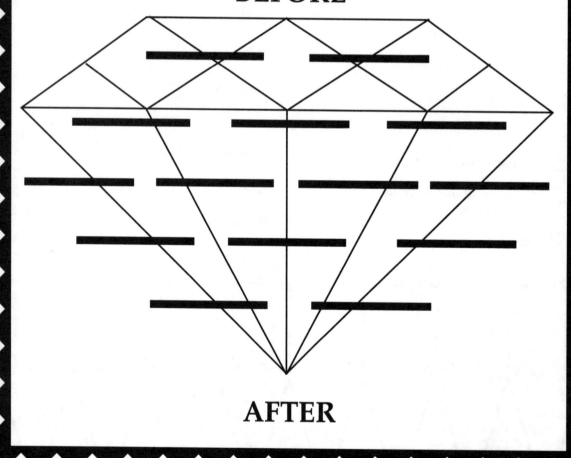

**BEFORE**

**AFTER**

© 1992 by The Standard Publishing Company.
Permission is granted to photocopy this page for ministry purposes only—not for resale.

# Eager Learners

## Worship Focus

Worship God because He teaches us through example and story.

## Transition Time

(5-10 minutes)

**Guessing Game.** Before the session, write simple tasks on slips of paper (folding a paper airplane, tying a shoe, washing a dish, and such). Divide the pupils into two teams. Pupils will take turns selecting a slip of paper and describing the task for their team. They may use no actions, only words. Set a time limit and award points when the team guesses correctly within the time limit.

## Launching the Theme

(5-10 minutes)

We just played a game in which you guessed an action only by hearing about it. But what if I showed you an action

and asked you to guess it? (Tie a bow with a piece of string or yarn. Fold an airplane, using a piece of paper. Ask pupils to guess what you are doing.)

It's easier to understand something when you can both see and hear about it, isn't it? If you are only hearing the directions, you can get confused. But when someone shows you what he wants, it's easier to understand.

God gave us His Word, the Bible, and He expects us to obey what we read. But we have more than an "instruction manual" to tell us how to live. When Jesus came to earth, He came first to die for our sins. But His life is also an example for us. Today we will worship God because He teaches us, not just in one way, but in many ways, especially through the example of Jesus.

## Building the Theme

(20-30 minutes)

**1. Call to Worship.** This group will compose a prayer, praising God for various characteristics of His teaching. Begin by giving each pupil a half sheet of paper and a pencil. **Do you remember a favorite teacher you have had? Write down several sentences telling why you admired the person and why you**

learned so much from him or her. **When you are choosing, don't just consider school teachers. Remember Sunday school teachers, piano teachers, coaches, camp counselors, or other special people in your life.** Allow several minutes for pupils to put their thoughts on paper. Then have them each share their ideas. Have a volunteer make a list on the chalkboard or newsprint of the character traits and teaching styles mentioned.

**Let's review this list of character traits and see how many of our favorite teachers are like God in some way.** Review the list, circling the words that could also be used to describe God as a teacher (such as patient, kind, fair, creative, caring). Then have students help you write a prayer. The prayer should praise God for the different traits you have discussed. Here is a sample:

We praise You, God, for being a patient teacher. You wait for us to learn, no matter how many times it takes.

We praise You, God, for being a teacher who gives examples of what You want. Thanks for sending Jesus to show us the kind of life to live.

We praise You, God, for being fair. Your rules are fairer than any others ever made. You do not have favorites.

We praise You, God, for being a compassionate and kind teacher. You know how to teach us and how to take care of us.

Ask each pupil or pair of pupils to choose one of the characteristics and write one sentence on that topic to include in the prayer. If your group is made up of older students, have them use a topical Bible or a concordance to find a Bible verse for each of the characteristics of God they decide to include.

**2. Devotion.** Pupils will investigate causes of spiritual death by reading Scriptures and summarizing the meaning on tombstones. Provide copies of activity page 8A, Bibles, and pencils. **Some people have a rather unusual hobby of visiting graveyards. It's not a morbid or spooky hobby. These people are there to read the old tombstones. The really old ones sometimes have interesting epitaphs on them. An epitaph is a saying short enough to carve on a tombstone. The saying is supposed to summarize the person's life. Some are sad, some are humorous. Today we are going to find out what happens to people who ignore teachings that God has for them.**

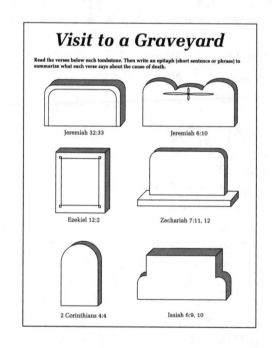

**Visit to a Graveyard**

Read the verses below each tombstone. Then write an epitaph (short sentence or phrase) to summarize what each verse says about the cause of death.

Jeremiah 32:33

Jeremiah 6:10

Ezekiel 12:2

Zechariah 7:11, 12

2 Corinthians 4:4

Isaiah 6:9, 10

Distribute activity page 8A with pencils and Bibles. Assign one or two Scriptures to each person. (If more than one person reads each Scripture, it will create more discussion.) Ask, **What does this verse mention that would have caused spiritual death?** (Look for answers such as stubbornness, hard heart, disobedience, spiritual deafness and blindness.) Then have students summarize their ideas by writing a short epitaph on the corresponding tombstone.

**3. Scripture.** This group will use an instant camera to prepare a "scrap book" showing examples of ways Jesus taught. You'll need a camera, film, scarves or robes to use as Bible costumes, some pieces of cardboard or construction paper and markers to make a few props or visuals, and a string or wire and some clothes pins for displaying the pictures.

Ask pupils to brainstorm a list of different ways, places, and times that Jesus taught people. Or have pupils read these Bible verses and discover who or how Jesus taught.

Matthew 4:23—teaching in a synagogue

Matthew 5:, 2—crowds on mountainside

Luke 7:39—personally teaching Mary and Martha

John 3:1—Nicodemus at night

John 4:4-26—Samaritan woman

John 7:14, 15—in temple courts

Matthew 12:46-50, John 10, 15—using visuals

Matthew 13:34, Luke 10:25-37—storytelling

Matthew 3:13, 15, John 13:4-17—by example

Then have pupils choose which Scripture accounts they will portray. Have them prepare any props needed. Then have pupils put on costumes and arrange themselves for the "snapshot." When the pictures are developed, attach them with clothespins to the string, or mount them on construction paper. Add captions to the pictures if you wish.

**4. Scripture.** This group will investigate Scriptures showing that God the Father, God the Son, and God the Holy Spirit are involved in teaching. They will prepare a song explaining this concept, as well as the idea that Christians are to be teachers also.

Distribute copies of activity page 8B, along with Bibles and pencils. Have students complete the verses and the mini-crossword puzzle. Review answers. **If God in three persons is involved in teaching us, what do you think that should tell us?** (1. God has a lot for us to learn. 2. God cares so much about us that all of Him is involved in helping us learn. 3. God uses many ways to reach us.) **What are ways we can make ourselves available to learn from God?** (Pay attention to parents, attend Sunday school and church, read the Bible, memorize Scripture, listen to Christian songs, pray for understanding). **What are ways we might—on purpose or accidentally—keep ourselves from learning from God?** (Ignore parents and teacher, skip Sunday school, fill mind with trash).

Lead pupils in choosing a way to present their information and discussion in the large group. They may wish to prepare a "Guess Who's Teaching Now" Game. They could make up clues and have other pupils guess. Or they could prepare a large copy of the crossword puzzle and have the large group complete it. Or they could compose a new verse to a familiar tune, highlighting the way that God, Jesus, and the Holy Spirit are all involved in teaching us. On the next page is an example of verses to tune of "God is So Good:"

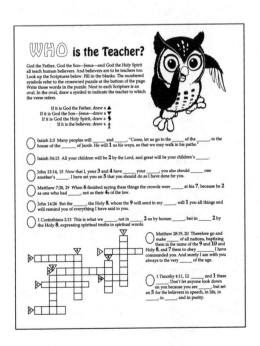

God is my teacher
He teaches all
His message goes out,
And we will have peace.

Jesus is my teacher
Authority is His
When I follow Him
I am pleasing God.

The Spirit is my helper
He is sent by God
He helps me remember
The words of God

I too will teach
All things He taught
By my example
Others will learn.

**5. Devotion.** This group will prepare skits about ways that students treat teachers. No materials are necessary, but you may wish to provide simple props.

**One way to praise God for teaching us and giving us teachers is to treat teachers in the right way. Our group will prepare a few skits to suggest right and wrong ways that students respond to teachers.** You may use the suggestions below, or ask pupils for their ideas. Have them select two or three ideas to enlarge into a brief skit.

1. *not paying attention to directions—* Tim is daydreaming while the teacher is giving directions for the assignment. He interrupts the teacher who is working with a student to ask questions about what to do.

2. *talking while teacher is trying to talk—* Jill and Leslie are whispering to each other and passing notes while the teacher is talking.

3. *not cooperating—* The substitute teacher asks the class where she can find the math papers they are supposed to do. The students know that the papers are in

a box on the shelf, but they pretend they don't know and say things like, "Maybe you should look in the desk."

4. *bring a small gift—* Terry brings her teacher a vase of flowers and says she is glad to be in this class.

5. *thank teacher for extra help—* Justin thanks the teacher for giving him special help with his math.

6. *being disrespectful—* Brian says, "This is really stupid. I don't want to play this dumb game," when the teacher introduces a new activity.

**6. Prayer.** This group will write a prayer, asking God to teach us, pledging our willingness to learn. Provide copies of activity page 8C, Bibles, and pencils or pens.

An Eager Learner's Prayer

Read the verses. Underline in each verse what the person is asking God to do for him. The verses are quoted from the *International Children's Bible.*

**Psalm 25:4, 5—** Lord, tell me your ways. Show me how to live. Guide me in your truth. Teach me, my God, my Savior. I trust you all day long.

**Psalm 27:11—** Lord, teach me your ways. Guide me to do what is right because I have enemies.

**Psalm 86:11—** Lord, teach me what you want me to do. And I will live by your truth. Teach me to respect you completely.

**Psalm 94:12—** Lord, those you correct are happy. You give them your teachings.

**Psalm 90:2—** Teach us how short our lives really are so that we may be wise.

**Psalm 119:33, 34—** Lord, teach me your demands. Then I will obey them until the end. Help me understand, so I can obey your teaching. I will obey them with all my heart.

**Psalm 143:10—** Teach me to do what you want, because you are my God.

**Job 34:32—** Teach me what I cannot see. If I have done wrong, I will not do it again.

Now read the verses again. Circle what the person says he will do in response to God.

Now write a prayer of your own, using ideas from the verses. Make the prayer personal and specific.

Have pupils read the Scripture verses printed at the top of the activity page. Underline in each verse what the person is asking God to do for him. Then read the verses again and circle the response of the person praying. What does that person hope to do or promise to do? Now look for this: Why does the person want God's help or teaching? There may be several answers to that.

Now let's prepare our own prayer,

drawing on these verses for ideas, but making the prayer personal for our group.

Allow pupils to work together to compose a prayer. Each pupil should write the prayer on his activity sheet.

**We will lead this prayer during the worship time, but first let's pray it together.**

# Sharing in Worship
● ● ● ● ● ● ● ● ● ● ● ● ● ● ● ●
**(20-30 minutes)**

Omit any of the following sections if you did not offer the corresponding activity.

**Call to Worship** (Group 1): **Group 1 compared God to their favorite teachers. Then they prepared this praise prayer, telling the qualities about God they appreciate.** Group 1 shows and prays aloud their prayer.

**Scripture** (Group 4): **Group 4 investigated some Scriptures to show how important teaching and learning are.** Group 3 presents their study through game, song, or interview, as they prepared.

**Music:** Sing "Father, I Adore You," including the verses "Jesus, I Love You . . ." "Spirit, I Adore You. . . ."

**Scripture** (Group 3): **Jesus is one of the best examples of a teacher. This group focused on the variety of ways that Jesus used to teach others. These pictures will give you an idea.** Group 3 shows their "photo album."

**Music:** Sing "The Teacher," "My Savior Teaches Me," or another song or hymn that carries the theme of Jesus' teaching.

**Lord's Supper:** The Lord's Supper is to us an object lesson—a reminder of Jesus and His teachings, and especially of His Sacrifice. Jesus taught His disciples that breaking the bread would remind us that His body was broken for us. The juice would remind us that He poured out His blood to pay for our sins. The Lord's Supper teaches us as we partake of it.

**Offering:** Jesus taught that "Where your treasure is, there your heart will be." That means your attitude toward material things is important if your heart is going to be right with God. Giving back to God in response to His many gifts to you shows your love and faith in Him.

**Devotion** (Groups 2 and 5): Bring a box you have wrapped and tied with ribbon to look like a gift. Inside the box put something valuable: some money or something delicious to eat.

**Jesus was a very unusual teacher. If we made a list of all His teachings we would have a very confusing list. Some teachings would be very simple and clear. Others would seem confusing. Perhaps you could interpret the meaning in several ways. Jesus prepared every teaching especially for the audience He had.**

**Some audiences were very hostile and angry, like the Pharisees. Jesus had harsh words for them.**

**Some audiences were very eager to obey Him. Jesus had clear and simple truths for them.**

**Some audiences were huge crowds of people. A few in the audience wanted to learn. Some only wanted to get a free meal or see a miracle. In those cases, Jesus taught in a clever way. He would tell a very interesting story, using examples people could easily relate to: farming, sheepherding, a lost coin. In each *parable* there was also a deeper meaning. Some in the audience just enjoyed the stories. Others wanted more. They saw beyond the story to its meaning. Or if they didn't quite get the idea, they stayed after class, so to speak, to ask Jesus about the meaning. Or they went home thinking, and came back later to ask Jesus if they had correctly figured out what He was saying.**

You might compare Jesus' style to this wrapped gift. The gift represents a teaching of Jesus. A few in Jesus' audience would hear what He said, but not appreciate it at all. Those would be the kind who would ignore a gift or just throw it away without opening it.

Others would focus totally on the outside: "Oh, isn't that a beautiful bow! Don't you love the color of the wrapping? Isn't the package wrapped and taped so carefully?" Those would never get around to focusing on the real meaning of Jesus' teaching, but see only the outside wrapping.

But some would look beyond the wrapping. They were the kind to wonder what would be inside. When they asked Jesus, He would open the gift for them—that is, He would explain more about what He had said. And when the gift was opened, it turned out to be much more valuable that the wrapping.

The Bible clearly shows that it is dangerous for a person to ignore God's teaching. Jesus' parable about the wise man and the foolish man illustrated what happens to a person who hears His teachings and does not obey them: the man's house was destroyed in a giant storm. Group 2 had the opportunity to visit a graveyard and read the tombstones of some who did not choose to obey God. Let's hear what they found. Have Group 2 share their tombstones.

Ask members of Group 5 to come forward and present their skits. **Did you ever think that one way to praise God might be the way you treat your teacher?** Group 5 prepared some skits to stimulate your thinking in this direction.

**Prayer (Group 6):** Group 6 will lead us in a prayer of commitment, pledging our willingness to learn from God our teacher.

# Closing Moments
●●●●●●●●●●●●●●●●●
**(10-15 minutes)**

Provide note paper or thank-you cards. Have pupils write a note to a former teacher, thanking the teacher for his or her influence. Arrange to have the notes mailed or delivered in person.

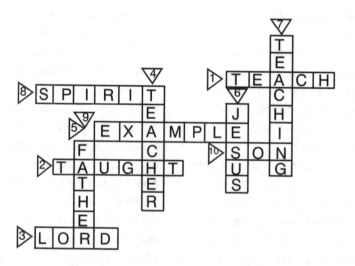

Answers to crossword puzzle on activity page 8B.

# Visit to a Graveyard

**Read the verses below each tombstone. Then write an epitaph (short sentence or phrase) to summarize what each verse says about the cause of death.**

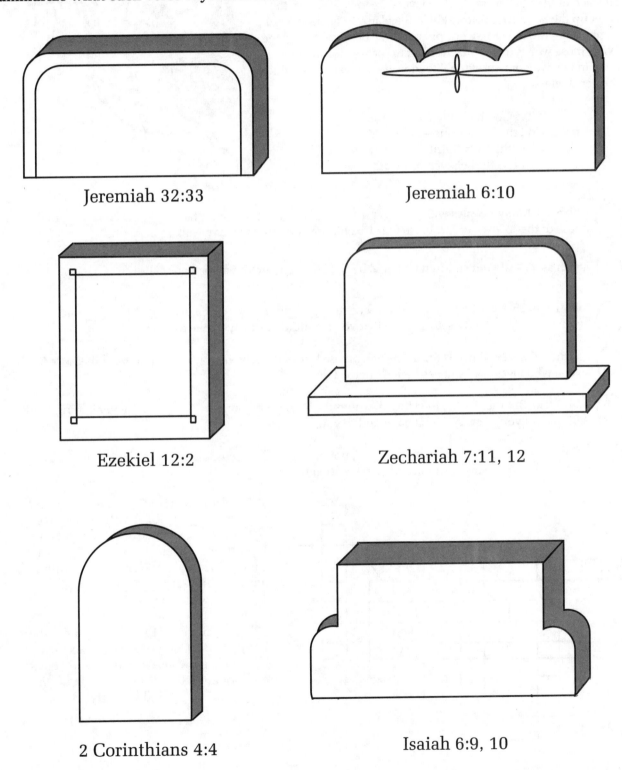

Jeremiah 32:33

Jeremiah 6:10

Ezekiel 12:2

Zechariah 7:11, 12

2 Corinthians 4:4

Isaiah 6:9, 10

© 1992 by The Standard Publishing Company.
Permission is granted to photocopy this page for ministry purposes only—not for resale.

# WHO is the Teacher?

God the Father, God the Son—Jesus—and God the Holy Spirit all teach human believers. And believers are to be teachers too. Look up the Scriptures below. Fill in the blanks. The numbered symbols refer to the crossword puzzle at the bottom of the page. Write those words in the puzzle. Next to each Scripture is an oval. In the oval, draw a symbol to indicate the teacher to which the verse refers.

If it is God the Father, draw a ▲
If it is God the Son—Jesus—draw a ▼
If it is God the Holy Spirit, draw a ⚡
If it is the believer, draw a ⚲

○ Isaiah 2:3  Many peoples will _____ and _____, "Come, let us go to the _____ of the _____, to the house of the _____ of Jacob. He will **1** us his ways, so that we may walk in his paths."

○ Isaiah 54:13  All your children will be **2** by the Lord, and great will be your children's _____.

○ John 13:14, 15  Now that I, your **3** and **4** have _____ your _____, you also should _____ one another's _____. I have set you an **5** that you should do as I have done for you.

○ Matthew 7:28, 29  When **6** finished saying these things the crowds were _____ at his **7**, because he **2** as one who had _____, not as their **4**s of the law.

○ John 14:26  But the _____, the Holy **8**, whom the **9** will send in my _____, will **1** you all things and will remind you of everything I have said to you.

○ 1 Corinthians 2:13  This is what we _____, not in _____ **2** us by human _____, but in _____ **2** by the Holy **8**, expressing spiritual truths in spiritual words.

○ Matthew 28:19, 20  Therefore go and make _____ of all nations, baptizing them in the name of the **9** and **10** and Holy **8**, and **7** them to obey _____ I have commanded you. And surely I am with you always to the very _____ of the age.

○ 1 Timothy 4:11, 12  _____ and **1** these _____. Don't let anyone look down on you because you are _____, but set an **5** for the believers in speech, in life, in _____, in _____, and in purity.

© 1992 by The Standard Publishing Company.
Permission is granted to photocopy this page for ministry purposes only—not for resale.

# An Eager Learner's Prayer

Read the verses. Underline in each verse what the person is asking God to do for him. The verses are quoted from the *International Children's Bible*.

**Psalm 25:4, 5**—Lord, tell me your ways. Show me how to live. Guide me in your truth. Teach me, my God, my Savior. I trust you all day long.

**Psalm 27:11**—Lord, teach me your ways. Guide me to do what is right because I have enemies.

**Psalm 86:11**—Lord, teach me what you want me to do. And I will live by your truth. Teach me to respect you completely.

**Psalm 94:12**—Lord, those you correct are happy. You give them your teachings.

**Psalm 90:2**—Teach us how short our lives really are so that we may be wise.

**Psalm 119:33, 34**—Lord, teach me your demands. Then I will obey them until the end. Help me understand, so I can obey your teaching. I will obey them with all my heart.

**Psalm 143:10**—Teach me to do what you want, because you are my God.

**Job 34:32**—Teach me what I cannot see. If I have done wrong, I will not do it again.

Now read the verses again. Circle what the person says he will do in response to God.

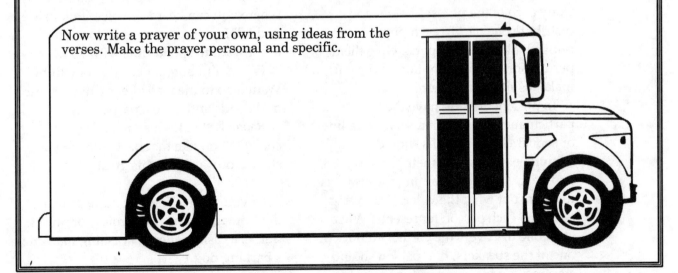

Now write a prayer of your own, using ideas from the verses. Make the prayer personal and specific.

© 1992 by The Standard Publishing Company.
Permission is granted to photocopy this page for ministry purposes only—not for resale.

# Listening Hearts

## Worship Focus
● ● ● ● ● ● ● ● ● ● ● ● ● ● ● ●

Worship God because He speaks to you.

## Transition Time
● ● ● ● ● ● ● ● ● ● ● ● ● ● ● ●
**(10-15 minutes)**

Before the session contact eight pupils and ask them to participate in an opening skit. Prepare a name tag for each participant by using yarn and a strip of paper. Have participants turn over the name tags so that their identity is concealed at the beginning of the skit. Copy each of the phrases below and distribute one part to each pupil. Have pupils look over their parts. Give them permission to change or add to the part to make it suitable for them.

To present the skit, have the participants arrange themselves in a line or semicircle. The pupils should simultaneously speak their parts over and over. Ask the remaining pupils to try to figure out what the voices are saying and who each person represents. When someone discovers the correct identity of one of the speakers, that person should stop reciting his part and turn over his name tag. Continue until each "voice" has been identified.

Here are the parts for the skit participants:

*Stomach:* You are hungry. Go directly to the refrigerator. You should eat something. Let's go find some junk food.

*Television:* Watch me. I'll entertain you. You don't want to miss the next episode of this exciting program.

*Parent:* Clean your room. Put your bike away. Don't fight with your sister. Turn down your loud music.

*Teacher:* Do your homework. Don't chew gum. Study for the test. Now we'll have a quiz.

*Advertisement* (or *Commercial*): You need this. Buy this. Spend your money here. This color would look great on you.

*God:* This is God speaking. Come away where you can hear My voice. Talk to Me, and tell Me your concerns. I love you, and I want to spend time with you.

*Friend:* I'm bored. Let's do something. Wanna go to the mall? Let's call up some of the kids and have a party.

*Radio:* Listen to this music. It's really cool. Do you like that beat? Maybe you should buy a CD of this great group!

(If you wish to include more pupils in the skit, add some extra voices or noises: traffic, a dishwasher or washing machine, a barking dog.)

# Launching the Theme

**(10 minutes)**

This skit represents our lives. Many voices and noises are clamoring for our attention. How were you finally able to hear what the voices were saying? (Let pupils respond.) It takes concentration, focusing in on one particular voice.

Perhaps it was a surprise to some of you that God wants to speak to you as much as He desires for you to pray to Him. You see, prayer is more than talking to God. Prayer also involves listening to Him. Today we'll see what the Bible says about how to listen to God. We'll look at Jesus' prayer life and see when He prayed and what kind of prayers He prayed. We'll review some different kinds of prayer and see which ones we use most often in our own prayer lives. Our goal today is to expand and balance our prayer life by learning more about praying and listening.

# Building the Theme

**(30 minutes)**

**1. Special Music.** Pupils will study hymns about prayer. You will need one hymnal for every two pupils. If you are a leader with limited musical ability, have a choir member and pianist make a tape, singing the first verse of each of these hymns: "What a Friend We Have in Jesus," "'Tis the Blessed Hour of Prayer," "Did You Think to Pray?", and "Sweet Hour of Prayer." Have pupils find each hymn in the hymnal before you play the tape. Pause the tape after each hymn. Ask pupils to summarize the message of the verse. Ask, **What feeling do you think** the writer was trying to communicate with these words? Does this song give an accurate representation of what the Bible teaches about prayer? Have pupils select one of these hymns to share during the worship time. (You may decide to use contemporary songs or choruses about prayer instead of traditional hymns.)

**2. Devotion.** Pupils will examine the prayers in Matthew 14 and compare themselves to the disciples. Provide copies of activity page 9A, Bibles, and pencils or pens. Have students skim over Matthew 14:22-33. Tell them to take note

of the different prayers included in the passage. List on the chalkboard or scratch paper the ones they mention. Then distribute the activity page, and have them work in pairs to complete it. After about eight minutes, review and discuss. Ask, **What are some crisis times in our lives when we forget to pray? Do you think you are more like Peter, a bold prayer person, or more like the disciples who failed to realize that Jesus could help them? Mark 6:51, 52 indicates that some of the disciples "slept through" the feeding of the 5000—that is, they did not gain an appreciation of Jesus' power.**

**When they saw Jesus walking on the water they were only frightened and amazed, not compelled to worship. What does Mark 6:52 say was the root of their trouble? What could you do to grow in your faith?** Have pupils prepare a summary of their study to present in *Sharing in Worship,* perhaps making a poster-size list of the four prayers.

**3. Devotion.** Pupils will complete a chart describing four kinds of prayer. They will evaluate their own prayers.

Before the session, divide a sheet of poster board into four sections. Label the four sections Adoration, Confession, Thanksgiving, Supplication. Copy the Scripture references below on strips of paper, one reference to a strip. Provide a dictionary for pupils to look up the four words. Invite them to write a definition on the poster. Distribute the Scripture slips. Have pupils find the verses, decide what kind of prayer they represent, and tape them to the poster in the correct category.

Then have pupils work together to write a prayer containing all four of the different kinds of prayer on the poster, perhaps one or two sentences from each. Explain that this prayer will be prayed during *Sharing in Worship,* so it should relate specifically to your class. For example, the confession part might say something like, "Father, we admit that sometimes we don't get serious about worshiping You." The supplication part might say something like, "Lord, help us to remember You during the week and worship You each day." Have the group select a song to be used with their prayer during the worship time.

Here are the Scripture verses to use, listed by category:

*Adoration:*
Psalm 145:1—"I praise your greatness, my God the King. I will praise you forever and ever."

Psalm 29:1, 2—"Praise the Lord's glory and power. Praise the Lord for the glory of his name."
Psalm 103:1—"My whole being praise the Lord. All my being, praise his holy name."
Psalm 30:1—"I will praise you, Lord, because you rescued me."

*Confession:*
Psalm 51:4—"You are the one I have sinned against. I have done what you say is wrong."
Psalm 32:5—"I will confess my sins to the Lord."
Psalm 41:4—"Lord, be kind to me. Heal me because I have sinned against you."

*Thanksgiving:*
Psalm 138:1—"Lord, I will thank you with all my heart."
Psalm 118:1—"Thank the Lord because he is good."
Psalm 105:1—"Give thanks to the Lord and pray to him. Tell the nations what he has done."

*Supplication:*
Psalm 71:12—"God, don't be far off. My God, hurry to help me."
Psalm 57:1—"Be merciful to me because I come to you for protection."
Psalm 26:2—"Lord, try me and test me. Look closely into my heart and mind."

**4. Prayer.** Pupils will read Bible verses about quiet and solitude to discover an essential ingredient for prayer. Provide copies of activity page 9B, Bibles, and pencils or pens. **When we teach about prayer, we describe it as simply talking to God. Sometimes we forget to tell you that prayer is more than talking. There is another essential ingredient. This puzzle will help you discover it.** Distribute copies of activity page 9B. Have pupils read the verses and fill in the blanks. The puzzle solution is SOLITUDE.

## The Essential Ingredient

Read the Scriptures below and fill in the missing word. Then transfer the numbered letters to the spaces below so you can discover an essential ingredient for prayer.

**1 Timothy 2:2** Pray for the leaders so that we can have _ _ _ _ _ _ and peaceful lives.

6

**1 Peter 3:4** Your beauty should come from within you—the beauty of a gentle and quiet _ _ _ _ _ _. This beauty will never disappear and it is worth very much to God.

1

**1 Thessalonians 4:11** _ _ _ _ all you can to live a peaceful life.

7

**Psalm 4:4** _ _ _ _ _ about these things quietly as you go to bed.

5

**Psalm 46:10** God says, "Be quiet and know that _ am God."

4

**Ecclesiastes 3:7** There is a time to be _ _ _ _ _ _ and a time to speak.

3

**Habakkuk 2:20** The Lord is in his Holy Temple. So all the _ _ _ _ _ should be silent in his presence.

8

**Zephaniah 1:7** Be silent before the _ _ _ _ _.

2

Your life needs _ _ _ _ _ _ _ _ because God's voice is
1 2 3 4 5 6 7 8

like a _____ (1 Kings 19:12).

How many minutes each day are you alone? _____

How many of those minutes alone are spent in a quiet place where you are not disturbed? _____

How many of those minutes are spent praying? _____

How many of those prayer minutes are spent listening, not talking, to God? _____

**Give God a chance to speak to you. Give yourself some solitude.**

Ask pupils to define solitude: "the quality or state of being alone or remote from society." Ask, **Why is solitude an essential ingredient for prayer?** Let pupils discuss. Stress that prayer includes listening to God as well as talking. God's voice is often drowned out (as the earlier skit portrayed) if our lives have no solitude. We receive God's answers by combining Bible study with our prayers, by receiving advice from other Christians, or by having the Holy Spirit give us thoughts or help us remember Bible verses we know. These are all ways that God speaks back to us. Most of them require that we take some uninterrupted time to reflect. Have pupils suggest ways to increase solitude in their personal lives. You may wish to write these on a poster to share during the large group time:

Schedule a definite quiet time.

Spend some time each day without background music.

Go for a walk.

Choose a regular spot where you won't be interrupted or distracted.

Read a Bible verse or paragraph.

Ask God to show you what you should learn.

Be quiet for a few moments and wait.

**5. Scripture.** Pupils will draw pictures to represent the different occasions when Jesus prayed. Provide sheets of newsprint and crayons, pencils, and markers. Assign each pupil to look up one or two of the verses listed below. If you want to make this activity more of a challenge, provide a concordance and have pupils find the Scriptures themselves instead of giving them the verses. Then have them prepare illustrations with captions, showing the various times when Jesus prayed.

Luke 5:16—many occasions in solitude
Matthew 14:23—alone from day until evening
Mark 6:41, 46—feeding the 5,000
Luke 22:41—in the garden
Luke 23:34—on the cross
Mark 1:35—healing multitudes
John 11:41—raising Lazarus
Luke 6:12—the transfiguration
Luke 9:29—at His baptism

**6. Scripture.** Pupils will match kinds of prayer to various prayers of Jesus. Distribute copies of activity page 9C, along with Bibles and pencils or pens.

Allow about five minutes for pupils to search the Scriptures. Then review the answers. **The Bible tells of many times**

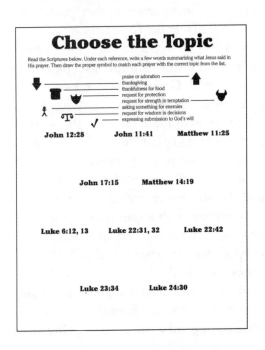

## Choose the Topic

Read the Scriptures below. Under each reference, write a few words summarizing what Jesus said in His prayer. Then draw the proper symbol to match each prayer with the correct topic from the list.

praise or adoration
thanksgiving
thankfulness for food
request for protection
request for strength in temptation
asking something for enemies
request for wisdom in decisions
expressing submission to God's will

**John 12:28**     **John 11:41**     **Matthew 11:25**

**John 17:15**     **Matthew 14:19**

**Luke 6:12, 13**     **Luke 22:31, 32**     **Luke 22:42**

**Luke 23:34**     **Luke 24:30**

Jesus prayed without always telling what He prayed about. We do know that He had a habit of regular prayer. Which kind of prayer do you suppose He prayed most often? Why? (Let students discuss.)

How many of these different kinds of prayer do you use? Which do you use regularly, which less often? How could you plan to include in your prayer life some of the prayers that you don't normally use? Have students prepare a report or chart to share the information about Jesus' prayers with the large group.

# Sharing in Worship
● ● ● ● ● ● ● ● ● ● ● ● ● ● ● ●
(20-25 minutes)

Omit any section if you did not offer the corresponding activity.

**Call to Worship.** Combine several of these commands to pray: 2 Chronicles 7:1; Philippians 4:6, 7; Ephesians 6:18; 1 Thessalonians 5:17; James 5:13; Matthew 26:41; 1 Timothy 2:1-3.

**Special Music** (Group 1): Have Group 1 share the song or songs they prepared during *Building the Theme.*

**Scripture** (Group 5): We'll begin by looking at Jesus' example as a person who prayed. Group 5 has prepared pictures illustrating different occasions when Jesus prayed. Group 5 shows their pictures and explains what they have learned about Jesus' prayers.

**Scripture** (Group 6): Have you ever had the strange experience of being in a prayer time with a group of friends and hearing a person give a "misplaced prayer," that is, one that didn't fit the occasion? Maybe the person thanked God for food when it wasn't mealtime, or prayed for a sick friend when you were supposed to be praising God for

something. This kind of thing happens because often we don't teach about the different kinds of prayer. So today we are going to dig a little deeper. Group 6 also studied Jesus and His prayers. Their focus was to discover the kinds of prayers He prayed. Have the report from Group 6.

**Devotion** (Group 3): There is still another way to learn about different kinds of prayer. Group 3 explored four kinds of prayer that are found in the Bible. Have them show their poster. The first letters of these words form an acrostic—that is, they spell a word, ACTS (Adoration, Confession, Thanksgiving, Supplication). Some people use this word to help them remember these four kinds of prayer. God wants to hear all of these kinds of prayer from us.

Group 3 has prepared their own prayer, including all four kinds. You might wonder if the prayer counts with God, since it was written out ahead of time and because it was an "assignment." It depends. Their prayer is meant to be offered as a prayer from all of us. If your heart and mind are tuned in to God as the prayer is prayed, then it is a prayer from you too. And even though it was written out, and has a specific format, God is pleased with the prayer.

Sing an appropriate song, then have the group present the prayer.

Next, provide 3" x 5" cards and pencils for pupils to make their own copy of the chart, writing in the four kinds of prayer. Ask them to circle the prayer they use most frequently. Ask pupils to tell which one they circled. Discuss ways for them to expand their prayers by praying other kinds of prayers. Have them write down on the back side of the card one or two helpful suggestions from the discussion.

**Lord's Supper:** When Jesus and His disciples had been  especially busy teaching and healing people, Jesus would say, "Come away for a while and rest." In our busy weeks, the Lord's

Supper is the same kind of invitation. It is a meal shared with a close friend, Jesus. It is meant to be a time to talk to Him, but also a time to listen. During the Lord's Supper, Jesus says, "Look at this table. Remember what I did for you. Remember that you are forgiven. Remember to come here when you need peace and strength."

Offering: We respond to God with open hearts in prayer, as we talk to Him and listen to Him. Now we will have the opportunity to respond to Him as we bring Him our offering.

Devotion (Group 2): Our starting place for today's focus on prayer was originally the account of Peter and Jesus walking on the water in Matthew 14. If we asked you to read this section of Scripture and choose a title for it, you might have called it "Peter's Great Faith," or "Jesus Stops the Storm." But it is also a story about prayer—several prayers, to be exact. Have Group 2 present their summary. Ask, If someone were reading a history of your life, would it resemble this Bible story, having places where you should have prayer and didn't?

Prayer (Group 4): We have talked about prayer as talking to God. But prayer is more than talking. There is another essential ingredient. Members of Group 4 discovered this ingredient and will share with us what they learned. After Group 4 is finished, introduce the prayer time.

This will be a quiet time, where you can think about your own conversations with God and talk to Him about what you need to do to improve communication with Him. Ask Him to remind you of your need for solitude and to help you make prayer a priority.

# Closing Moments
**● ● ● ● ● ● ● ● ● ● ● ● ● ● ●**
**(10-15 minutes)**

In the ACTS formula for balancing prayers, *Thanksgiving* and *Supplication* probably come naturally to your pupils. *Confession* is no doubt more difficult, especially aloud in a group. But *Adoration* is the area in which many Christians, even adults, have difficulty.

Lead a discussion with your pupils about Adoration in prayers. Explain it something like this: **In Thanksgiving, we talk to God about what He does: Thank You, God, for doing such and such, or giving such and such." But in Adoration, we praise God for who He is: "God, I love You because You are . . ." "I honor You because . . ." We tell God what He means to us.**

Help the pupils come up with ideas for things they can include in their prayers, differentiating between Adoration and Thanksgiving.

# 4 Prayers

Read Matthew 14:22-33, and answer the questions below.

**Jesus' Prayer**
*Matthew 14:23*
What do you think Jesus might have prayed about? Check these verses.
John 6:15
Matthew 14:12, 13

**The Missing Prayer**
*Matthew 14:24, 25*
Who forgot to pray? What should they have prayed about?
Mark 6:49, 50
John 6:18, 19

**Peter's Prayer of Faith**
*Matthew 14:30, 31*
What did Peter pray? Why?

**The Disciples' Prayer**
*Matthew 14:33*
How did the disciples respond to what they witnessed? Did all the disciples respond the same way? Read Mark 6:51, 52.

List all the different kinds of prayer you discovered in your research.

When you learn remarkable things about Jesus, how do you respond?
a. "Yawn. No big deal."
b. "Interesting. I'll have to think about that someday."
c. "I love You, Lord. I want to serve You."

© 1992 by The Standard Publishing Company.
Permission is granted to photocopy this page for ministry purposes only—not for resale.

# The Essential Ingredient

Read the Scriptures below and fill in the missing word. Then transfer the numbered letters to the spaces below so you can discover an essential ingredient for prayer.

**1 Timothy 2:2** Pray for the leaders so that we can have _ _ _ _ _ and peaceful lives.
6

**1 Peter 3:4** Your beauty should come from within you—the beauty of a gentle and quiet _ _ _ _ _ _ _. This beauty will never disappear and it is worth very much to God.
1

**1 Thessalonians 4:11** _ _ all you can to live a peaceful life.
7

**Psalm 4:4** _ _ _ _ _ about these things quietly as you go to bed.
5

**Psalm 46:10** God says, "Be quiet and know that _ am God."
4

**Ecclesiastes 3:7** There is a time to be _ _ _ _ _ _ and a time to speak.
3

**Habakkuk 2:20** The Lord is in his Holy Temple. So all the _ _ _ _ _ should be silent in his presence.
8

**Zephaniah 1:7** Be silent before the _ _ _ _.
2

Your life needs __ __ __ __ __ __ __ __ because God's voice is
1  2  3  4  5  6  7  8

like a _____ (1 Kings 19:12).

How many minutes each day are you alone? _____

How many of those minutes alone are spent in a quiet

place where you are not disturbed? _____

How many of those minutes are spent praying? _____

How many of those prayer minutes are spent listening, not talking, to God? _____

**Give God a chance to speak to you. Give yourself some solitude.**

© 1992 by The Standard Publishing Company.
Permission is granted to photocopy this page for ministry purposes only—not for resale.

# Choose the Topic

Read the Scriptures below. Under each reference, write a few words summarizing what Jesus said in His prayer. Then draw the proper symbol to match each prayer with the correct topic from the list.

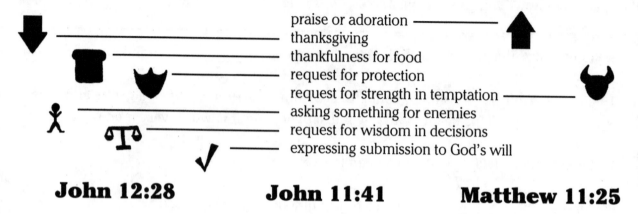

praise or adoration
thanksgiving
thankfulness for food
request for protection
request for strength in temptation
asking something for enemies
request for wisdom in decisions
expressing submission to God's will

**John 12:28**          **John 11:41**          **Matthew 11:25**


**John 17:15**          **Matthew 14:19**


**Luke 6:12, 13**          **Luke 22:31, 32**          **Luke 22:42**


**Luke 23:34**          **Luke 24:30**

© 1992 by The Standard Publishing Company.
Permission is granted to photocopy this page for ministry purposes only—not for resale.

# Truthful Living

## Worship Focus
● ● ● ● ● ● ● ● ● ● ● ● ● ● ● ● ●

Worship God because He can always be trusted.

## Transition Time
● ● ● ● ● ● ● ● ● ● ● ● ● ● ● ● ●
(10-15 minutes)

Arrange your group in pairs or trios. Provide Bibles for approximately half of the pairs. Distribute copies of activity page 10A. Explain to the pupils that the point of this activity is to see what difference it makes when some have access to their Bibles and some do not.

For your information, here are the statements from the activity sheet, along with the answers:

a. The woman was surprised that Jesus would speak to her. (True: men did not usually speak to strange women in public and Jews did not speak to Samaritans if they didn't have to.

b. The woman told Jesus the truth when she said she had no husband. (True. She had previously been married 5 times, but now lived with a man to whom she was not married.)

c. The well originally belonged to Isaac. (False. It belonged to his son Jacob.)

d. Jesus offered the woman something better than water. (True. He offered her living water that would allow her never to be thirsty again.)

e. When Jesus began to tell the woman about her personal life, she changed the subject. (True. She diverted the conversation to, "Where should we really worship?"

f. Jesus criticized the woman for her loose morals. (False. He didn't criticize her. He just stated truth.)

g. God wants worshipers who worship

TRUE • FALSE • TRUE • FALSE • TRUE • FALSE • TRUE • FALSE • TRUE • FALSE • TRUE • FA
LSE • TRUE • FALSE • TRUE • FALSE • TRUE • FALSE • TRUE • FALSE • TRUE • FALSE • TRU
E • FALSE • TRUE • FALSE • TRUE • FALSE • TRUE • FALSE • TRUE • FALSE • FALSE

### WHAT'S THE TRUTH?

Write a T for true and an F for false in the blanks below. The verses in parentheses refer to John, chapter 4.

____ a. The woman was surprised that Jesus would speak to her (verse 9).

____ b. The woman told Jesus the truth when she said she had no husband (verses 17, 18).

____ c. The well originally belonged to Isaac (verse 6).

____ d. Jesus offered the woman something better than water (verses 13 14).

____ e. When Jesus began to tell the woman about her personal life, she changed the subject (verses 19, 20).

____ f. Jesus criticized the woman for her loose morals (verses 17, 18).

____ g. God wants worshipers who worship Him in spirit with sincerity (verse 24).

____ h. Jesus criticized the Samaritans for not worshiping in Jerusalem (verse 21).

____ i. The woman got mad at Jesus and returned to town (verses 28, 29).

Write a word that describes your feeling about this activity, such as confident, frustrated, contented, or disgusted:

_____

Circle the method you used to complete the quiz:

checked Bible for correct facts

relied on memory

asked someone else's opinion

Him in spirit with sincerity. Sincerity usually means with wholehearted or genuine feeling. God wants truth, not feelings.)

h. Jesus criticized the Samaritans for not worshiping in Jerusalem. (False. He said soon the time was coming when people wouldn't worship only on Mt. Gerazim or in Jerusalem. God cares more about the hearts of the worshipers than the place where they worship.)

i. The woman got mad at Jesus and returned to town. (False. She returned to town to tell people that she believed Him to be the Messiah. She was not mad.)

After about ten minutes, review the answers, asking with each question, **In what verse did you find the answer to that question?** Then say, **Did those of you without a Bible feel frustration? Of course, because the other groups could check their answers. They didn't have to depend on their memory or their opinions.**

**The point of this quiz was not to show us that it's easier to pass the quiz if you can look in the Bible. The point is about truth. Life is like this quiz. There are always questions to answer. Sometimes you know the answer, sometimes you may think that you know the answer. But a Christian can always find the answer by checking with the source of truth: the God of the Bible. Nonbelievers have nothing to use as a guide to "check their answers." They are left to follow their feelings or their opinions or follow someone else's advice. We are not so helpless or hopeless, because we know the source of truth. Today each one of us will try to answer this question: Since God is truth, how should I live in a way that pleases Him?**

# Launching the Theme
•••••••••••••••••••
(5 minutes)

**Worship requires knowing God as He truly is. He isn't glorified when we have the wrong information about Him. For example, in some ancient cultures people offered babies as sacrifices, because they had false information about who the one true God is and what pleases Him.**

**God isn't glorified when we have the wrong information about how to worship Him. For example, some religions teach people to worship God by hurting their bodies, cutting or whipping themselves. But the God of the Bible has never commanded people to torture themselves to atone for their sins. He sent His own Son Jesus as the sacrifice for all.**

**God isn't glorified when we don't know His Son. For example, some people believe it doesn't matter who people worship—Jesus, or Buddha, or Muhammad. These people think they're all about the same. But of course we know that only Jesus is God in human form. He is more than a great teacher or prophet—He is God himself.**

**God wants worshipers who seek truth: truth about God, about Jesus, and about themselves. God wants worshipers who live by the truth. How can we find that truth? We find it in the Bible by reading it, studying it, and listening to others who are doing the same.**

# Building the Theme
•••••••••••••••••••
(30 minutes)

**1. Call to Worship.** Pupils will prepare and practice a call to worship about truth.

Provide Bibles, a large sheet of newsprint, and markers.

Have pupils find these verses. Ask, **What does this tell us about God and truth?** The answers are given below for your reference.

John 17:17—His word is truth
Psalm 19:9—His judgments are true
Psalm 117:2—His truth is everlasting
Hebrews 6:18—It is impossible for God to lie
Jeremiah 10:10—The Lord is the true God
Isaiah 45:19—I am the Lord, and I speak the truth. I say what is right

Next, have pupils find these verses. Ask, **What does God want us to do about truth?**

Psalm 86:11—Teach me . . . and I will live by your truth
Psalm 51:6—You want me to be completely truthful
Philippians 4:8—Think about truth
Ephesians 4:15—Speak the truth lovingly
1 Corinthians 13:6—Rejoice in truth
Psalm 51:6—Have truth in our hearts
Zechariah 8:19—Love the truth
2 Timothy 2:15—Handle accurately His Word of truth

Have pupils select verses or phrases they wish to include in their call to worship. One possible format is to prepare the call to worship as a responsive reading. After each sentence about God, include one of the verses telling how God wants us to live. Have pupils write these on the newsprint, in lettering large enough for the whole group to read. Then have the group practice reading the verses together aloud.

**2. Special Music.** Pupils will write new words to a familiar song on the theme of truth. Provide paper, pencils, and if you wish, a songbook or two.

Have pupils select a familiar song and compose a new set of words, with the theme focusing on living a truthful life. "I Have the Joy, Joy, Joy," will work well with 3 John 3, 4. It might sound like this: **"It always gives me joy when I hear you are following the truth, following the truth, following the truth,"** and repeat. "Jesus Loves Me" will fit with 1 John 3:18. **"If you want to show true love, you must do more than just talk. Actions show you really love. Let true love show through your life."** Provide scratch paper to jot down sentences. Then have pupils copy the words on a large sheet of newsprint so they can teach the song during the worship time.

If time permits, or if your group is large, you may want to include this project in addition to writing a song: write a prayer to be used during the worship time, based on Psalm 25:4, 5, 26:2-4, 86:11.

**3. Scripture.** Pupils will match Scriptures about ways to be truthful and illustrate good and bad examples of those actions. You'll need 12 3" x 5" cards, drawing paper, and markers. Before the session copy each of these Scripture phrases and references on two of the cards:

God wants us to:

Think about truth—Philippians 4:8
Speak the truth lovingly—Ephesians 4:15
Rejoice in truth—1 Corinthians 13:6
Have truth in our hearts—Psalm 51:6
Love the truth—Zechariah 8:19
Handle accurately His Word of truth—2 Timothy 2:15

Shuffle the cards and spread them out on the table or floor. Have pupils take turns turning over two cards, trying to find a match. When all the cards are matched, ask pupils to suggest specific actions that would be a good or bad example of each of the Scriptures. Then ask pupils to volunteer to illustrate one or more of the ideas and include the Scripture reference at the bottom of the picture. Provide paper and markers. Have pupils prepare to explain their illustrations during *Sharing in Worship*.

**4. Devotion.** Pupils will prepare skits showing ways to live truthfully. You'll need to provide Bibles, and if you wish, scratch paper for writing notes or simple props for the skits.

Review these situations with the pupils. Brainstorm for possible good and bad solutions to each situation. Have pupils select several of their solutions to act out during *Sharing in Worship*. They may want to come up with their own situations. Ask, **What could happen if the person tells the truth? What could happen if the person lies? Is it still lying if the person doesn't actually have to say anything? Is it only a sin if the person gets caught? Why or why not?**

Here are some situations the pupils may use:

a. You didn't finish reading the book for a report that is due tomorrow. You are at a friend's house. She shows you her report. Do you use her information?

b. You are invited to a sleepover. Your friends are choosing a movie to watch. They ask you if you've already seen a certain one. You could say that you've already seen it. Or you could tell the truth and say that your parents won't allow you to see it.

c. Your neighbor hired you to weed her garden while she was away. Now she gets out her wallet and asks, "How many hours did it take you?" You could exaggerate just a little to get some extra money.

d. You "borrowed" a tape of your brother's without asking. It got ruined. Now your brother asks you if you've seen his missing tape.

e. The baby-sitter's boyfriend comes over. (Your parents don't allow that.) They take you out for ice cream and beg you not to tell your parents. The next morning your mom says, "I tried to call last night. Were you all outside?"

If you have time, discuss Bible people who told the truth when it was dangerous to do so:

*Joseph*—told the Pharaoh the dream about the coming famine, told the baker he would die, told his brothers about his dreams of being greater than them

*Esther*—told the king that she was a Jew

*Micah*—told Ahab the king that he would die in battle, got slapped

*John the Baptist*—told Herod it was wrong for him to take his brother's wife

**5. Scripture.** Pupils will prepare warning signs about the results of lying. Before the session use construction paper to cut out shapes of traffic signs. Ask pupils what the signs are used for. They warn drivers of hazards coming up in the road, a stop, or dangerous curve. Explain that pupils will find Bible verses that give warnings about the danger of lying. Have pupils look up verses, talk about what they mean, and choose which ones to write on warning signs.

*Proverbs 12:9*—Lies last only a moment, but truth endures forever.

*Proverbs 12:22*—The Lord hates those who tell lies.

*Proverbs 19:5*—A witness who lies will be punished.

*Proverbs 21:6*—Wealth that comes from telling lies vanishes like a mist and leads to death.

*Proverbs 23:23*—Learn the truth and never reject it!

*Psalms 5:6*—You destroy liars. The Lord hates those who kill and trick others.

*Psalm 63:11*—The mouths of liars will be shut.

*Revelation 21:8*—But those who are cowards, who refuse to believe, who do evil things, who kill, who sin sexually, who do evil magic, who worship idols, and who tell lies—all these will have a place in the lake of burning sulfur. This is the second death.

Have pupils prepare to show and tell about their warning signs during *Sharing in Worship*.

**6. Devotion.** Pupils will discuss examples of people worshiping and set goals for improving their own personal worship. Provide copies of activity page 10B. Read through the situations with the group. After each one ask, **Is this person worshiping in spirit and in truth? Why or why not? What needs to happen to make the worship more truthful?** When you have discussed each situation, have pupils choose three they would like to present to the large group. Then have them complete the bottom section of the activity page where they set goals for

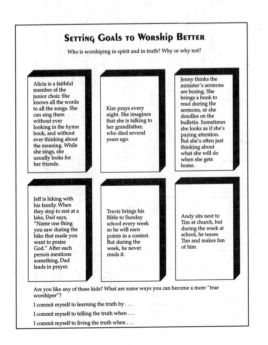

themselves to improve their own worship. Ask them to share one or more of their goals and write them on a sheet of newsprint or a blank transparency to give as possible examples during *Sharing in Worship*.

# Sharing in Worship
**(20-25 minutes)**

Omit any section if you did not offer the corresponding activity.

**Call to Worship** (Group 1): **We worship God because He can be trusted. He is truth, and everything He says or does is truthful. The best response we can make to Him is to worship Him in spirit and truth.**

Group 1 reads the call to worship they prepared.

**Scripture** (Group 3): What does the Bible tell us about how to live truthfully? Group 3 has some illustrations of these ideas. Have pupils show and explain the illustrations they made.

**Special Music** (Group 2): Have pupils sing the song they wrote, then teach it to the large group.

**Scripture** (Group 5): **What happens when a person doesn't live truthfully? The Bible tells about that too. Group 5 will share what they discovered.** Have members of Group 5 show the warning signs they prepared, explaining the Scriptures they read.

**Lord's Supper: You've probably heard the old saying, "You can fool some of the people all of the time, and you can fool all of the people some of the time, but you can't fool all of the people all of the time." I believe this is true. But an even more important truth is this: You can never fool God, but you can fool yourself. Jeremiah 17:9 says that a**

person's heart is deceitful. He can never trust himself completely. He can never be objective. That's why it is so great to know and trust God. He is always completely truthful. First Corinthians 11:28 says that the Lord's Supper is a time for a person to "examine himself." That means to be completely truthful with yourself. Admit your failures. Admit your mistakes. Ask God to help you see yourself as you are. After you've looked at yourself, then look at the Lord's Table: the bread and the juice remind you that all your sins are forgiven through Jesus.

**Offering:** When we worship through bringing our offering, it is a good opportunity for us to tell ourselves the truth about our material possessions. If we think too highly of our possession, giving an offering will probably be difficult for us. Giving cheerfully is evidence that we have the proper attitude toward possessions.

**Devotions** (Groups 4 and 6): Before the session cut out letters from construction paper using the pattern on page 96. Apply tape or plasti-tak to the back of the letters.

Answer to the maze puzzle, activity page 10C.

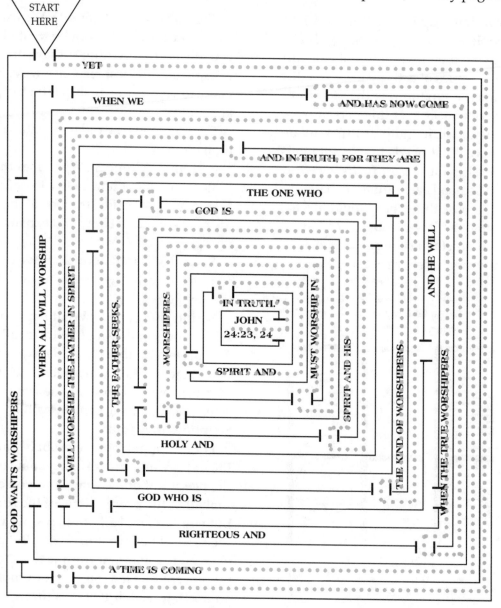

What makes truth so important? Why is it essential to life? One answer must be that Jesus said, "I am the truth," and "The truth will make you free."

This first T will stand for the cross, the place where Jesus paid for all the wrong and false actions of all people. His death wipes out the sins.

The R will stand for right, or righteous. When you try to describe or explain truth, you use words like reality, accuracy, actual, honesty, genuine, authentic. Truth is a starting place for life. It gives us a road map to go by, a foundation to build on.

Let's skip the U for a moment, and focus on the TH. The Greek word for God is *Theos*. We'll have this TH stand for God, because God is truth, just as Jesus is. We heard from the Bible that His ways are true, His words are true, His works are true. His love and His plan provided for Jesus to give His life to make us free. The truth in His Word shows us how we can live truthfully.

Now the U, in the middle, right where it belongs. The U of course, represents you. When you follow God's truth, you are surrounded by truth. You are on a foundation of truth. You are protected and supported. The first part of the Christian armor in Ephesians 6 is the "belt of truth" Wearing this belt, or living a life based on God's truth protects you from the attacks of Satan, the father of lies. This U is surrounded, but not trapped. And that is precisely what God wants you to know. When you live by the truth, it does make you free.

Living truthfully is sometimes difficult. At some time in your life, maybe even this past week, you were faced with the decision to live by the truth or to act deceitfully. Group 4 has

selected several such situations for you to consider. See how what have decided to deal with the truth. Have Group 4 present the skits they prepared.

Group 4 challenged us to live our daily lives more truthfully. Group 6, meanwhile, was considering ways to make worship times more truthful. Group 6 presents their examples and shares possible goals for worshiping more truthfully.

**Prayer:** Have a pupil or assistant close in prayer, praising God for His truthfulness, and asking His help in living truthfully.

# Closing Moments
● ● ● ● ● ● ● ● ● ● ● ● ● ● ●
**(5-10 minutes)**

Distribute copies of activity page 10C so that each pupil has one. Provide Bibles and wide-tipped felt markers, and have pupils work through the maze by reading John 24:23, 24.

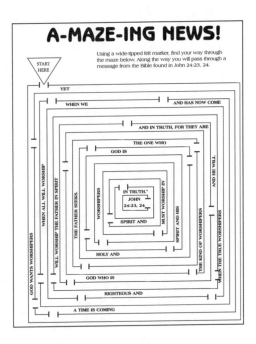

© 1992 by The Standard Publishing Company.
Permission is granted to photocopy this page for ministry purposes only—not for resale.

# WHAT'S THE TRUTH?

*Write a T for true and an F for false in the blanks below. The verses in parentheses refer to John, chapter 4.*

___ a. The woman was surprised that Jesus would speak to her (verse 9).

___ b. The woman told Jesus the truth when she said she had no husband (verses 17, 18).

___ c. The well originally belonged to Isaac (verse 6).

___ d. Jesus offered the woman something better than water (verses 13 14).

___ e. When Jesus began to tell the woman about her personal life, she changed the subject (verses 19, 20).

___ f. Jesus criticized the woman for her loose morals (verses 17, 18).

___ g. God wants worshipers who worship Him in spirit with sincerity (verse 24).

___ h. Jesus criticized the Samaritans for not worshiping in Jerusalem (verse 21).

___ i. The woman got mad at Jesus and returned to town (verses 28, 29).

Write a word that describes your feeling about this activity, such as confident, frustrated, contented, or disgusted:

_____

Circle the method you used to complete the quiz:

checked Bible for correct facts

relied on memory

asked someone else's opinion

© 1992 by The Standard Publishing Company.
Permission is granted to photocopy this page for ministry purposes only—not for resale.

# SETTING GOALS TO WORSHIP BETTER

Who is worshiping in spirit and in truth? Why or why not?

Alicia is a faithful member of the junior choir. She knows all the words to all the songs. She can sing them without ever looking in the hymn book, and without ever thinking about the meaning. While she sings, she usually looks for her friends.

Kim prays every night. She imagines that she is talking to her grandfather, who died several years ago.

Jenny thinks the minister's sermons are boring. She brings a book to read during the sermons, or she doodles on the bulletin. Sometimes she looks as if she's paying attention. But she's often just thinking about what she will do when she gets home.

Jeff is hiking with his family. When they stop to rest at a lake, Dad says, "Name one thing you saw during the hike that made you want to praise God." After each person mentions something, Dad leads in prayer.

Travis brings his Bible to Sunday school every week so he will earn points in a contest. But during the week, he never reads it.

Andy sits next to Tim at church, but during the week at school, he teases Tim and makes fun of him.

Are you like any of these kids? What are some ways you can become a more "true worshiper"?

I commit myself to learning the truth by . . .

I commit myself to telling the truth when . . .

I commit myself to living the truth when . . .

© 1992 by The Standard Publishing Company.
Permission is granted to photocopy this page for ministry purposes only—not for resale.

# A-MAZE-ING NEWS!

Using a wide-tipped felt marker, find your way through the maze below. Along the way you will pass through a message from the Bible found in John 24:23, 24.

START HERE

YET

WHEN WE

AND HAS NOW COME

AND IN TRUTH, FOR THEY ARE

THE ONE WHO

GOD IS

GOD WANTS WORSHIPERS

WHEN ALL WILL WORSHIP

WILL WORSHIP THE FATHER IN SPIRIT

THE FATHER SEEKS.

WORSHIPERS

IN TRUTH."

JOHN 24:23, 24

MUST WORSHIP IN

SPIRIT AND HIS

AND HE WILL

THE KIND OF WORSHIPERS

WHEN THE TRUE WORSHIPERS

SPIRIT AND

HOLY AND

GOD WHO IS

RIGHTEOUS AND

A TIME IS COMING

© 1992 by The Standard Publishing Company.
Permission is granted to photocopy this page for ministry purposes only—not for resale.

# Unselfish Giving

## Worship Focus

Worship God because He is generous.

## Transition Time

**(10-15 minutes)**

Provide paper and pencils for pupils. Give these instructions: **Name five items you purchased for yourself or received as gifts in the last six months. Are each of these items more important or less important to you than when you received them? (Next to each item on the list, answer "More" or "less.") If you had it to do over again, are there any you wouldn't buy or wouldn't ask for? Why or why not?** Discuss briefly. **Sometimes in the heat of the moment we think we must have a certain thing—because everyone else has it, because it will make us feel more accepted, or for many other reasons. Then as time passes, we discover that the thrill of owning this important gotta-have-it thing has passed away. We find we didn't need it as much as we thought, or it didn't live up to its reputation. What can we do to help us get a grip on ourselves and our thirst for possessions?**

## Launching the Theme

**(10 minutes)**

**Raise your hand if the category I mention applies to you. These are ways you may have used money last week:**

> bought a food or snack item
> bought something for myself
> saved for a special item I want
> spent money on entertainment
>   (movie, skating, miniature golf)
> lent money to a friend
> gave to God through my church
> gave to God by helping the poor
> shared a good item with a friend
> shared a possession or item of
>   clothing with a brother or sister
> gave away something of mine.

**Money, money, money! What does money have to do with your relationship to God? Today we are going to look at the answer to that question. We're going to recall gifts we've received from God. We're going to list some principles for handling money, advice from people who used their money wisely, and advice from people who weren't so wise. Our goal today is to stretch our idea of ways that we can like God through being generous with our money. We will worship God because He generously gives all things.**

# Building the Theme

● ● ● ● ● ● ● ● ● ● ● ● ● ● ●

## (30 minutes)

**1. Devotion.** Pupils will prepare and practice a skit about using money. Before the session contact several pupils and ask them to bring items like these, representing things that kids this age would typically shop for: shoes, sport items, shirts or jackets, tapes or CDs, toys, skates, videos, and such. Try to collect approximately one item for each pupil in the small group.

Explain that the skit will portray a person going shopping. In this particular situation, the price tags talk. That is, they give the shopper advice about whether or not she should purchase the items. Your skit may have more than one shopper, perhaps a boy and a girl. You'll need a table on which to place the items, and a large blanket or tablecloth to cover the table so pupils can hide under it. You'll also need paper, markers, and tape for preparing the price tags.

**What would happen to a shopper if, as he shopped, the various items he looked at actually spoke to him, telling him what they were really worth? What kinds of things would the shopper hear?** Jot down pupils' suggestions. Look for ideas like these:

"You'll play with this for three days and get bored."
"These shoes will wear out in three months."
"This [clothing item] will be out of style by fall."
"You don't really need this."
"You can get along without this."
"The batteries will run down and you'll never use it again."
"This will break the second time you use it."
"If you wait a month, this will be on

sale. By then you probably won't even want it."
"This has no eternal value."

The one or two pupils playing the parts of the shoppers do not speak. They simply move along the sale table, handling the items. The rest of the pupils choose one line to say from their spots underneath the table, as if the sale items were speaking to the shoppers. When the shoppers have looked at and listened to all the items, have them leave the store without purchasing anything. Have the hidden actors recite together this paraphrase of Matthew 6:19, 32, 33; "Don't buy for yourselves treasures here on earth. The clothes wear out and the things break. You heavenly Father knows what you need. Seek God's kingdom first. Then you have all the other things you need."

If your group is advanced, you may ask them to select some Bible verses to use at the end of the skit. Provide a concordance.

**2. Personal Praise.** Pupils will prepare a review of the gifts God has given. *(Note: You may want to have two groups working on this project.)* Provide 24 boxes, wrapping paper, tape, and ribbon. You'll need about 40 pieces of paper, pencils, markers, or crayons.

Assign each pupil one or more letters of the alphabet. Have her find the Scripture, discover what gift from God is listed in that verse; and then copy the verse across the bottom of the paper. Pupils may highlight the word that names the gift, and draw a picture illustrating it. If there is time to do so, have them put their papers inside a box, close, and gift wrap it. If your time is short or if your class is large enough to be using most of the other suggested activities, you may need to skip the wrapping part. Instead, have pupils use whole sheets of construction paper, fold them in half, and write the Bible verse and draw the gift inside. Then they can attach ribbon and a bow or decorate the outside of the paper as if it were a gift box. Then pupils will only need to fold up the paper to reveal the gift, instead of taking the time to unwrap the box.

Here are the Scripture verses to assign. Unless otherwise indicated, they are taken from the *International Children's Bible*. For your reference only, answers are given in parentheses.

A Romans 8:32 (all things)
B 2 Corinthians 9:8 (blessings)
C Revelation 2:10 (crown of life)
D Psalm 37:4, *NASB* or *KJV* (desires of heart)
E James 1:17 (everything good)
   Romans 15:5 (everything good)
F Acts 14:17 (food)
G Psalm 85:12 (goodness)
   1 Timothy 1:14 (grace)
H Galatians 1:4 (himself)
   Romans 15:13 (hope)
   Jeremiah 24:7 (heart to know me)
I Genesis 1:26 (image of God)
J Acts 14:17 (joy)
K Daniel 1:17 (knowledge)
   Psalm 84:11 (kindness)
L John 10:28 (eternal life)
   1 Peter 1:3 (living hope)
M Isaiah 41:27 (messenger)
   Romans 11:32 (mercy)
N John 13:34 (new commandment)
   1 Peter 1:3 (new life)
O John 3:16 (only begotten Son)
P Romans 15:13 (peace)
   Romans 15:5 (patience)
Q Psalm 23:2 (quiet waters)
R Acts 14:17 (rain)
   Psalm 23:2 (rest in green pastures)
S 2 Corinthians 5:5 (spirit)
   Psalm 29:11 (strength)
T 1 John 3:22 (things we ask for)
U 2 Timothy 2:7 (understanding)
V 1 Corinthians 15:57 (victory)
W 1 Corinthians 3:5 (work to do)
   James 1:5 (wisdom)
   Revelation 21:6 (water of life)

**3. Offering.** Pupils will investigate the cost of their Sunday school materials and supplies. They will prepare a mock bill. Before the session, obtain a copy of these items: your annual church budget, a curriculum order, and a price sheet from a school supply catalog or store. Also have on hand copies of activity page 11C, pencils and, if you wish, a calculator or two for pupils to use.

### Can You Pay the Bill?

Church attendance is free to everyone! But it does cost something. Have you ever wondered how much it costs for your congregation to provide the facilities, materials, and supplies for you and your friends? Here's a worksheet to help you figure the cost.

**SUNDAY SCHOOL CURRICULUM**
cost of one pupil book
cost of take-home paper for one pupil
cost of teacher book
cost of visual aids
TOTAL ____ x 4 quarters per year =

**FACILITIES**
yearly cost of utilities
yearly salary of custodian
yearly insurance premiums
yearly cost of building or mortgage
TOTAL ____ divide by 2 because half this cost is for adults, half for children =

**SUPPLIES (YEARLY TOTALS)**
Miscellaneous (pencils, paper, glue)
Music
Refreshments (including social activities)
Vacation Bible School
Video rental or purchase
Puppets
camp scholarships
TOTAL ____ write total in box=

**SALARIES**
Children's minister
Youth minister
TOTAL ____ write total in box=

Add all numbers in boxes; write total here.
Divide the number in the ◯ by the total number of persons under the age of 18 in your church. Write that number here.

The number in the ◇ presents the amount of money spent by your congregation each year on each person under the age of 18.

Begin by giving each pupil small slips of paper and a pencil. **How much money do you suppose this church spends on you each year?** Ask pupils to brainstorm some of the ways that the church spends money on them. Then have them write down their estimate of the total. Collect these and read aloud, having a volunteer write down all the guesses. Then distribute copies of activity page 11C. Show the copies of the budget and other information you brought. Help the pupils work through the activity sheet to find out approximately how much the church spends each year for Sunday school and other children's activities. Compare the actual amount of the estimates from pupils. How close did they come? Have them copy the information onto a large sheet of newsprint or a transparency so that the information can be displayed during *Sharing in Worship.*

You can make this activity more dramatic by giving each pupil a large amount of play money. As your group figures the total for each section of the worksheet, appoint a "bill collector" to receive that amount of money from each pupil.

**4. Scripture.** Pupils will complete a crossword puzzle and be able to state advice from Proverbs about money. Provide copies of activity page 11A, pencils or pens, and copies of the *International Children's Bible.* When pupils have finished the puzzle, review the answers by having them take turns reading the completed proverbs. Ask them why they think the proverb gives true advice. Have them select five principles to share during the large group time. Draw a large hand on a sheet of newsprint. Have pupils write out the principles on the fingers of the hand and refer to this visual as they present it during *Sharing in Worship.*

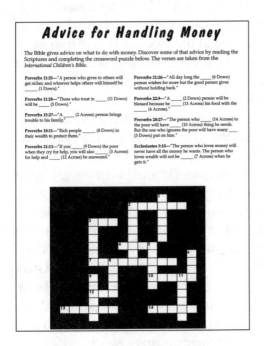

If your group normally uses the *New International Version* or *King James Version,* you may choose to have pupils prepare their own crossword puzzles. Provide

graph paper. Before the session write out a list of about ten Bible verses on the subject of money, or use the ones on the activity page. Instruct pupils to use the top half of their graph paper to plan their puzzles. A puzzle consisting of five to seven words is about the right length. Then have them prepare a blank puzzle and trade with another member of the group. Save time for reviewing principles and planning how to present them during *Sharing in Worship.*

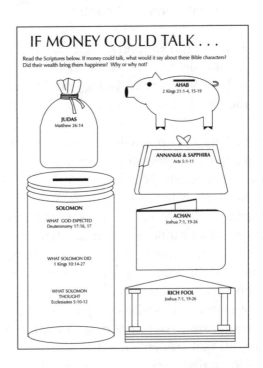

**5. Scripture.** Pupils will read about Bible characters and write down how they showed stinginess or greed. **Have you ever heard the expression, "money talks"? The idea is that you can tell a lot about a person if you can see how he gets money or spends it. Today we're going to look at several Bible characters and imagine that their money is telling us about them.** Distribute copies of activity page 11B. Assign each pupil to find and read the Bible verses about one of the characters listed. Then discuss: How did this person get his wealth? What did this person do with his wealth? If this person's use of money could give us some advice for today, what would it be? Jot notes on scratch paper during the discussion. Then have pupils write out the advice from the character they researched. (Some pupils may be working on the same character.) Have pupils prepare to share their "advice" during the large group time.

> Ahab—Kings 21:1-4, 15-19
> Solomon—what God expected: Deuteronomy 17:16, 17; what Solomon did: 1 Kings 10:14-27; 11:1-6; what Solomon thought: Ecclesiastes 5:10-12
> Ananias and Sapphira—Acts 5:1-11
> Achan—Joshua 7:1, 19-26
> Judas—Matthew 26:14-16; John 12:4-6
> Rich Fool—Luke 12:16-21

**6. Scripture.** Pupils will prepare a matching game to review Bible people who gave generously. You'll need 16 4" x 6" cards or sheets of construction paper, plus Bibles, pencils, and markers. Assign pupils one or more Scriptures. After finding the Scripture, have them write on one card the name of the person or group who gave something, and the Scripture reference that describes the gift. On the second card have pupils draw a picture of the gift that was given.

When that is completed, collect the cards. Shuffle them and arrange them face up on the table or floor. Have pupils take turns trying to match the giver with the gift he or she gave.

Here are the Scriptures to assign, and for your reference only, the gifts and givers the pupils should identify:

> Luke 23:50-53—Joseph of Arimathea gave Jesus his own new tomb
> Mark 12:41-44—Widow gave two small coins
> John 6:9-12—Boy gave two fish, five loaves
> Romans 15:26; 2 Corinthians 8:1-5—Macedonians collected money for famine in Jerusalem

> John 12:3-8—Mary gave expensive perfume to Jesus
> Ezra 6:8-10, 12—Darius, King of Medes, gave supplies to rebuild and run the new temple (sheep, wheat, salt, wine, oil)
> Acts 4:32-35—Early Christians sold land or houses to help others
> Exodus 35:20-29—Israelites gave gold jewelry and other gifts for building the tabernacle
> Acts 4:36, 37—Barnabas sold some land and gave money to apostles

# Sharing in Worship
● ● ● ● ● ● ● ● ● ● ● ● ● ●
## (20-25 minutes)

Omit any section if you did not offer the corresponding activity.

**Call to Worship:** Have pupils read aloud Matthew 6:19-21 as a group.

**Scripture** (Groups 4, 5, and 6): **Where is your treasure? We'll be considering that question today. We'll begin by looking at the lives of two different groups of Bible people: some who were generous with their possessions, and some who were not.**

Have Group 5 present their advice from the money bags of stingy or greedy Bible characters.

Then have Group 6 lead the group in matching up Bible givers with the gifts they gave. Then ask, **What do we learn from the examples of these two groups of people?** Jot down suggestions on a sheet of newsprint or chalkboard. **Group 4 discovered specific Scriptures about handling money. Let's see if our ideas match up with theirs.** Have Group 4 present their findings.

**Music:** Sing "Take My Life, and Let It Be," "We Give Thee But Thine Own," or other appropriate songs.

**Personal Praise** (Group 2): **We have**

focused on what we are supposed to do with our belongings. But we need to go back a step. Why are we supposed to be generous? Will God be pleased if we give away our stuff, but inside we are only giving because the Bible says we should? The Bible says, "God loves a cheerful giver." So what will make you cheerful about being generous? Perhaps this presentation from Group 2 will spark your interest. Group 2 presents the gifts from God.

Lord's Supper: Perhaps if every week we had a demonstration and reminder of God's many gifts we would feel like being generous. In a way we already do have that—in the Communion service. A we eat, we taste and touch juice and bread to remind us of God's greatest gift to us. salvation through the death of His Son. What a costly gift!

Offering (Group 3): Have Group 3 display the bill they prepared. This represents the approximate amount of money that our church spends on each of you every year in order to provide you with Sunday school material, a building to meet in, and activities to help you grow. Does it surprise you to know that the church cares enough to gladly spend this money on you? Would you and your family be surprised if you received a bill from the church saying, "Please pay for the supplies you have used and the services you have received"? That would be a shock wouldn't it?

More than that, what if God sent you a bill for all those many things He has done for you? You couldn't pay if you spent your entire life working two jobs. No problem, however, because salvation and all that comes with it is free. No price tag, no bill. God doesn't command us to pay for what we have received. Instead the Bible commands us to be generous, to share with others, to give gladly. "God loves a cheerful giver; freely you have received, freely give."

God says that when we give to Him we will receive a great blessing.

When you eat at a restaurant with your family, it is the custom to leave a tip. The tip is a small token for the waitress or waiter, a way of showing appreciation for the service given.

When you consider what the church spends on you each year, does it seem as though you are giving enough? Are you only paying for what you are receiving: lessons, pencils, markers, papers? Are you only tipping, leaving a small token of appreciation? Or are you a sacrificial giver, one who gives to God with joy? Early in the session we reviewed ways we had spent our money recently. Although the Bible doesn't tell us how much to give, it does encourage us to evaluate our giving. We are to give regularly, to give proportionately. That means we plan ahead, we don't just give God whatever is left over at the end of the week. We start with Him. And we do it because we love Him, not because we must. Will you evaluate your gifts to God as we sing this song and receive our offering? Sing "Freely, Freely," or another appropriate song.

Devotion (Group 1): We begin our time together by recalling things we bought and examining our attitudes toward money. Those activities don't seem like worship. Surely it is more spiritual to read Bible verses about handling money and to thank God for His gifts to us. Those are acts of worship. But there are other acts of worship just as pleasing to God: actions that take place when we make choices about how we will spend the money we do have. Group 1 has prepared a skit. Try to imagine yourself as the shopper. Have Group 1 present their skit.

Prayer: Ask a pupil or assistant to close the session in prayer, praising God for His generosity and asking His help in developing a cheerful attitude toward giving.

Answers to crossword puzzle, activity page 11A.

# Closing Moments

● ● ● ● ● ● ● ● ● ● ● ● ● ● ●

**(5-10 minutes)**

On the chalkboard or a sheet of news-print write,

Got it?

Give it:

Get it:

Provide pupils with half sheets of paper and pencils, and ask them to copy the three phrases. Next to *Got it?* jot down several of the gifts from God that you appreciate the most. Next to *Give it:* write down two or three ways you can be more generous with what you have—not only your possessions and money, but also your time and your abilities. Next to *Get it:* describe what rewards or satis-faction you will receive from following this action plan, such as knowing you are pleasing God, and knowing you are growing as you learn to share.

# Advice for Handling Money

The Bible gives advice on what to do with money. Discover some of that advice by reading the Scriptures and completing the crossword puzzle below. The verses are taken from the *International Children's Bible*.

**Proverbs 11:25**—"A person who gives to others will get richer, and whoever helps others will himself be _____ (1 Down)."

**Proverbs 11:28**—"Those who trust in _____ (11 Down) will be _____ (5 Down)."

**Proverbs 15:27**—"A _____ (2 Across) person brings trouble to his family."

**Proverbs 18:11**—"Rich people _____ (8 Down) in their wealth to protect them."

**Proverbs 21:13**—"If you _____ (9 Down) the poor when they cry for help, you will also _____ (3 Across) for help and _____ (12 Across) be answered."

**Proverbs 21:26**—"All day long the _____ (6 Down) person wishes for more but the good person gives without holding back."

**Proverbs 22:9**—"A _____ (2 Down) person will be blessed because he _____ (13 Across) his food with the _____ (4 Across)."

**Proverbs 28:27**—"The person who _____ (14 Across) to the poor will have _____ (10 Across) thing he needs. But the one who ignores the poor will have many ____ (3 Down) put on him."

**Ecclesiastes 5:10**—"The person who loves money will never have all the money he wants. The person who loves wealth will not be _____ (7 Across) when he gets it."

© 1992 by The Standard Publishing Company.
Permission is granted to photocopy this page for ministry purposes—not for resale.

# IF MONEY COULD TALK . . .

Read the Scriptures below. If money could talk, what would it say about these Bible characters? Did their wealth bring them happiness? Why or why not?

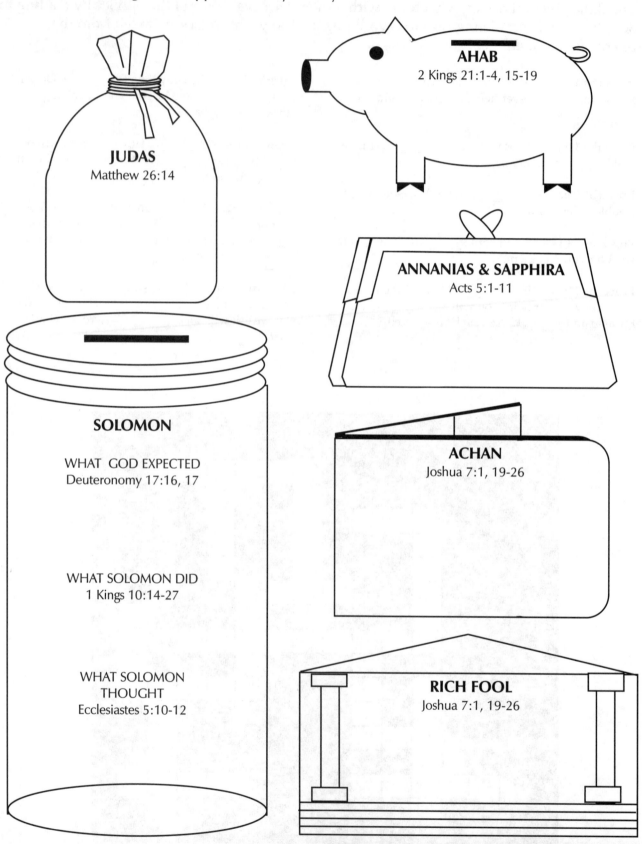

**JUDAS**
Matthew 26:14

**AHAB**
2 Kings 21:1-4, 15-19

**ANNANIAS & SAPPHIRA**
Acts 5:1-11

**SOLOMON**

WHAT GOD EXPECTED
Deuteronomy 17:16, 17

WHAT SOLOMON DID
1 Kings 10:14-27

WHAT SOLOMON
THOUGHT
Ecclesiastes 5:10-12

**ACHAN**
Joshua 7:1, 19-26

**RICH FOOL**
Joshua 7:1, 19-26

© 1992 by The Standard Publishing Company.
Permission is granted to photocopy this page for ministry purposes only—not for resale.

# Can You Pay the Bill?

Church attendance is free to everyone! But it does cost something. Have you ever wondered how much it costs for your congregation to provide the facilities, materials, and supplies for you and your friends? Here's a worksheet to help you figure the cost.

**SUNDAY SCHOOL CURRICULUM**

| | |
|---|---|
| cost of one pupil book | _____ |
| cost of take-home paper for one pupil | _____ |
| cost of teacher book | _____ |
| cost of visual aids | _____ |
| **TOTAL** | _____ x 4 quarters per year = ☐ |

**FACILITIES**

| | |
|---|---|
| yearly cost of utilities | _____ |
| yearly salary of custodian | _____ |
| yearly insurance premiums | _____ |
| yearly cost of building or mortgage | _____ |
| **TOTAL** | _____ divide by 2 because half this cost is for adults, half for children = ☐ |

**SUPPLIES (YEARLY TOTALS)**

| | |
|---|---|
| Miscellaneous (pencils, paper, glue) | _____ |
| Music | _____ |
| Refreshments (including social activities) | _____ |
| Vacation Bible School | _____ |
| Video rental or purchase | _____ |
| Puppets | _____ |
| camp scholarships | _____ |
| **TOTAL** | _____ write total in box= ☐ |

**SALARIES**

| | |
|---|---|
| Children's minister | _____ |
| Youth minister | _____ |
| **TOTAL** | _____ write total in box= ☐ |

Add all numbers in boxes; write total here. ◯

Divide the number in the ◯ by the total number of persons under the age of 18 in your church. Write that number here. ◇

The number in the ◇ presents the amount of money spent by your congregation each year on each person under the age of 18.

© 1992 by The Standard Publishing Company.
Permission is granted to photocopy this page for ministry purposes only—not for resale.

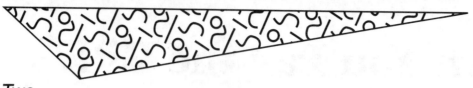

# Joyful Serving

## Worship Focus

Worship God because He gave His Son as a servant.

## Transition Time

(10-15 minutes)

As pupils arrive have them write their names on slips of paper and place the slips in a basket. Then draw out two names. The first will be "King or Queen for a Day," and the second will be "Servant for a Day." Have a tray of snacks ready for the servant to bring, a pillow, footstool, cloth for polishing shoes, or other equipment to use while serving. Provide a bell for the king to ring when he wants the servant to do something. Move on to the next activity quickly, but instruct the king that he is free to tell the servant to do something for him while the session continues.

## Launching the Theme

(10 minutes)

Play Wheel of Fortune or Hangman. Have all the puzzles be titles for Jesus: Prince of Peace, Isaiah 9:6; Christ, Matthew 16:16; Lord of Lords, Revelation 19:16; Head of the Body, Colossians 1:18; King of Kings, Revelation 19:16. Then have the final title be Servant, Matthew 12:18. **It is not difficult for us to remember that Jesus is the Lord and King of our lives. We know that He is our Savior, but sometimes we forget that the way He became our Savior was by becoming a servant to all. Today we are going to explore places in the Bible where Jesus is called a servant, as well as check out ways that He served others. We will find out the attitudes God wants us to have as we serve Him, and discover what kinds of rewards servants should expect.**

## Building the Theme

(30 minutes)

**1. Scripture.** Pupils will formulate a list of attitudes God wants servants to have, and will prepare coupons offering their

## Servanthood Coupons

Read the Scriptures and supply the missing words. Then fill out the servanthood coupons with the names of people you will serve, and the tasks you will do to serve them. Remember to sign the coupons, cut them apart, and present them to the people for whom you made them.

**SERVANTHOOD COUPON**
In Galatians 5:13 Christians are told to ____ each other with. I will show love as I ____ for you. Presented to ____ Signed ____

**SERVANTHOOD COUPON**
Ephesians 6:7 says to work as if you were ____ the ____ I will ____ for you as if I were doing it for Jesus. Presented to ____ Signed ____

**SERVANTHOOD COUPON**
The Bible says to ____ the ____ with all your heart (Romans 12:11). I will ____ with all my heart because I'm serving the Lord too. Presented to ____ Signed ____

**SERVANTHOOD COUPON**
In Psalm 100:2 I read, "____ the ____ with ____." I will joyfully ____ with ____. Presented to ____ Signed ____

**SERVANTHOOD COUPON**
I learn in 1 Peter 4:11 that the person who serves should ____ with the ____ that ____ for you with the strength that God gives me. I will ____ for you with the ____. Presented to ____ Signed ____

**SERVANTHOOD COUPON**
Second Corinthians 9:7 says, "God loves a ____." I will cheerfully ____ for you. Presented to ____ Signed ____

---

### A Servant/A King

Check out these Scriptures and fill in the blanks.

**Isaiah 42:1**—God calls Jesus His _____ and says He is _____ with Jesus.

**Acts 3:13**—God gives _____ to Jesus, who is _____ _____.

**Matthew 20:28**—Jesus did not come _____, but Jesus came to _____ others.

**Luke 22:27**—Jesus said He is like a _____.

**Philippians 2:7**—Jesus made himself _____, taking the _____ of a _____. He became _____.

Compose a prayer.

1. Write a sentence telling who God is and who we are.
   God, You are the _____ and we are your servants.
2. Write a sentence praising God for making a plan to save us.
3. Write a sentence praising Jesus for becoming a servant to us.
4. Write a sentence describing ways that Jesus served us.
5. Write a sentence describing your feelings.
   When I think of how You have served us, I feel _____
6. Write a sentence of commitment, telling God that you want to serve Him.
7. Write a sentence describing one way you will serve Him.

---

read Scriptures about Jesus being a servant and then compose a prayer of praise and commitment. Provide Bibles and scratch paper and copies of activity page 12B. Have pupils read the five Scripture verses listed at the top of the activity page and fill in the blanks. Select

service to others. Prepare enough copies of activity page 12A for the entire group. Group 1 will distribute them during the worship time. Begin with a graffiti wall. Place a sheet of newsprint on the wall. Across the top write, "What two chores do you dislike most?" Have pupils take turns writing their answers. Then have them tell why they dislike a particular chore more than others. **Is there someone you like to help or serve? Why do you like to serve that person? Is there someone you dislike helping? Why? Do you resent doing chores you don't get paid for? Should you always expect to be rewarded for your service?** Talk about what happens in a family when parents assign a chore, but children perform the chore with a bad attitude.

Distribute the activity sheets, and have each pupil find one of the Scriptures. Have them identify the attitudes God wants servants to have. Make a list of these on your graffiti wall. Have pupils discuss whom they would like to serve and fill out the servanthood coupons on their own activity pages. Have pupils prepare to share the list of attitudes during *Sharing in Worship.*

**2. Call to Worship/Prayer** This group will

one of the verses as a call to worship and ask a volunteer to read it aloud during the worship time. Then have pupils work individually to write a prayer. After about five minutes, ask each person to share his. Then select a sentence from each person to create a group prayer. Write this on scratch paper. You may need to reword it to apply to the entire group. Select someone to pray the prayer during *Sharing in Worship.*

**3. Scripture.** Pupils will discover ways that Jesus served others and brainstorm ways that they can serve others. Provide copies of activity page 12C, and have pupils decode the phrases. Have them check their answers in Bibles. Also provide Bible story books with large pictures, old teaching pictures, or Bible school visuals. Ask pupils to locate pictures of Jesus that illustrate the decoded phrases. During *Sharing in*

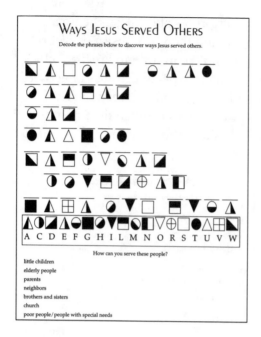

**Ways Jesus Served Others**

Decode the phrases below to discover ways Jesus served others.

A C D E F G H I L M N O R S T U V W

How can you serve these people?

little children
elderly people
parents
neighbors
brothers and sisters
church
poor people/people with special needs

*Worship* they will show the pictures when they share what they learned.

Then ask each pupil to brainstorm ways to serve someone in each of these categories: little children, parents, siblings, elderly people, neighbors, church, poor or needy in your town.

**4. Scripture.** Pupils will study six Bible characters who were too proud. Provide Bibles and 3" x 5" cards on which you've written the names and Scripture references listed below, one to a card. Assign each pupil to read the Scripture about one person and discover how that person displayed his pride. Then have them tell the consequences.

Write out these words from Romans 12:3 on 3" x 5" cards, one word to a card: DO NOT THINK YOU ARE BETTER THAN YOU REALLY ARE. Scramble the cards. Give one or two to each pupil. Have them try to arrange the cards in the correct order. When they think they have the answer, provide a Bible and the Scripture reference for them to check. Discuss: **Why would this Bible verse have been good advice for these Bible characters we've just studied? How can we keep from being too proud to serve others?**

Here are the Bible characters to use:

Pharaoh (Exodus 5:2, 12:29; 14:27, 28)—refused to let God's people go; son died; killed when God closed the Red Sea

Uzziah (2 Chronicles 26:16)—offered incense on an altar (a priest's job) and was struck with leprosy; although kind, had to live the rest of his life in seclusion

Haman (Esther 3:5)—angry when Mordecai wouldn't bow to him; tried to destroy all of God's people; eventually hung on the gallows he had prepared for Mordecai

Nebuchadnezzar (Daniel 4:30)—took all credit and glory for his achievements; God took his power and forced him to live like a wild animal for seven years

Herod (Acts 12:21-23)—people called him a god; he did not give glory to God; he was eaten by worms

**5. Thank-you Notes.** This group will write notes to thank people who have served them in various ways. Provide cards and envelopes or note paper. Or have your group make thank-you cards. These should be directed to people in the church who have served them in some way: former Sunday school teachers, youth group sponsors, ministers, people who clean the church building, drivers, and such.

Begin by giving each pupil paper and pencil. Ask, **How many people would you guess have in some way served you and your class this year?** Have pupils suggest numbers. **Write down as many names as you can. If you don't know a person's name, just write down how that person served you. Let's see how close your guesses come to the actual number. And let's see who can remember the most people who served you.** You may want to give some suggestions about the types of service you're looking for so kids don't write down "waiter at McDonald's."

After several minutes, review each person's list. Then ask each pupil to choose one name on the list and write a thank-you note. Decide if you want to send these from individuals or have the entire group sign them.

**6. Devotion.** This group will review Bible teaching about rewards for serving. They will illustrate verses and present them in a "commercial" format.

**When a person becomes a follower of Jesus, that person is committing himself to be a servant. A Christian must be willing to serve all people at all times and in all ways. Whether or not people thank us or praise us, or even notice what we are doing, God wants us to be servants.**

**The good news, however, is that servanthood has its reward. Let's check out some Bible verses to see exactly what kind of reward we can expect. Then we will use our findings to prepare some "commercials" or "advertisements" that explain the benefits of being a servant.**

Assign a Bible verse to each pupil. Have pupils find the verses and read them, looking for what the verse tells about reward. Some verses list specific kinds of reward. Other verses simply promise that God will reward. Discuss the findings. You may wish to compile a list on the chalkboard or on scratch paper as you discuss. Then have pupils select which verses they wish to illustrate. Provide sheets of newsprint and markers. Have pupils decide what to say to advertise the reward mentioned in that verse. They can write down what they will say on the back of the illustration. Have them practice presenting their commercials.

Here are verses to use (quoted from the *International Children's Bible*):

Matthew 10:42—"Whoever helps one of these little ones because they are my followers will truly get his reward. He will get his reward even if he only gave my follower a cup of cold water."

Matthew 19:29—"Many who have the highest place in life now will have the lowest place in the future. And many who have the lowest place now will have the highest place in the future."

Matthew 25:23—"The master answered, 'You did well. You are a good servant who can be trusted. You did well with small things. So I will let you care for much greater things. Come and share my happiness with me.'"

Matthew 6—"Be careful! When you do good things, don't do them in front of people to be seen by them. If you do that, then you will have no reward from your Father in heaven."

Luke 6:35—"So love your enemies. Do good to them, and lend to them without hoping to get anything back. If you do these things, you will have a great reward. You will be sons of the Most High God."

Ephesians 6:8—"Remember that the Lord will give a reward to everyone, slave or free, for doing good."

Colossians 3:23, 24—"In all the work you are doing, work the best you can. Work as if you were working for the Lord, not for men. Remember that you will receive your reward from the Lord, which he promised to his people. You are serving the Lord Christ."

Hebrews 6:10—"God is fair. He will not forget the work you did and the love you showed for him by helping his people. And he will remember that you are still helping them."

Revelation 22:12—"Listen! I am coming soon! I will bring rewards with me. I will repay each one for what he has done."

# Sharing in Worship

● ● ● ● ● ● ● ● ● ● ● ● ● ● ●

## (20-25 minutes)

Omit any section if you did not offer the corresponding activity.

**Call to Worship** (Group 2): Have the volunteer read the verse selected by the small group.

**Music:** Sing "If You Wanna Be Great in God's Kingdom" (from *Kid's Praise 4),* or other appropriate songs your pupils know.

**Scripture** (Group 3): **The best example we have for serving others is Jesus himself. Group 3 looked at some of the ways that Jesus served others.** Group 3 presents their pictures of visuals and reviews ways Jesus served others.

**Scripture** (Group 4): **Now we turn our attention from the best example in the Bible of serving to some of the worst. Here is a glimpse of a few people who should have served others, but didn't because they were too proud.** Have Group 4 summarize.

**Scripture** (Group 1): **Sometimes it is not what you do for others, but the attitude you have while performing the service that makes your service a true form of worship. Group 1 discovered some of the attitudes we need for service.** Have Group 1 review the Scriptures and distribute the servanthood coupons.

At this time, ask the "King/Queen for a Day" and "Servant for a Day" selected during *Transition Time* to come forward. Talk to them about their experience during the session. Ask the servant, **How did you feel while serving the king (queen)? What kind of master was he? What would the ideal master be like?** Ask the queen (king), **How did you feel being served? What would the ideal servant be like? What did you learn through your experience about God and serving Him?** Let the master and servant speak first, then allow other pupils comment on what they observed.

**Lord's Supper:** Display a towel and basin or bowl of water. **These two items are often used as symbols of Jesus' service to others. They recall the time that He washed the disciples' feet. When we focused on the bread and the juice of the Lord's Supper, these too should remind us of another service Jesus performed for us: paying the price for our sins with His own blood and body.** Read Romans 5:8.

**Offering: We usually ask for volunteers to collect the offering, and we consider that a way to serve both God and our worship group. But today let's concentrate on everyone serving. We'll put an offering plate here in front. Please come forward quietly to bring your offering, and then return to your seat.**

**Devotion** (Group 6): **The Bible teaches us to keep on being servants whether or not we are thanked or appreciated or rewarded. But the Bible also teaches us to expect that God will ultimately reward us for our service to others. Group 6 will give you a preview of your coming reward.** Group 6 presents their "commercials."

Before the session, fill out a set of the servanthood coupons (activity page 12A) with good deeds you might do for others. Place these in your pocket.) **Imagine that you are standing at the gate of Heaven. God says, "Why should I let you come in? What have you done for Me?" Would you pull out of your pocket your collection of handy-dandy servanthood coupons as a record of your good deeds? Let's see (pull out one), you visited a sick person. Oh, don't forget the time you shoveled your neighbor's sidewalk (pull out another). You helped rake leaves at a widow's yard. Maybe you sharpened the pencils in the pew racks every week for a year.**

How many of these coupons would you need to show God before He would say, "Stop, I think that's enough good deeds. Now you can enter My Heaven." Let pupils respond. The answer is NONE. You don't need any evidence of your good deeds to enter Heaven. After all, God can see everything you do, and He has a good memory. So when you get there, He'll just let you come in, right? Yes, He will allow you to come right in, but not because of your service.

Heaven is offered to those who have believed that Jesus is God's Son, and have obeyed His Word. Jesus paid the entrance fee when He died on the cross. You get to go in because of what Jesus did, not because of any good service you ever do for anyone else.

We have read Scripture verses today that tell us to serve others, and to do so cheerfully and wholeheartedly. But we serve others because we love God, not because we want to go to Heaven.

Prayer (Group 2): Group 2 has prepared a prayer of praise and commitment. Let's all join them in prayer.

After the prayer, wrap up the session by saying, **As a result of this study and praise, I hope you will commit yourself to serving others in a joyful, faithful way. But another result could be that our group would pledge ourselves to finding some ways to help and serve others. Group 3 brainstormed some possible ways to serve others. Let's listen to their ideas and see if we can choose one that might become a class project.** Also have Group 5 share the letters they wrote, and have others sign them if appropriate.

# Closing Moments
## (5-10 minutes)

Have pupils complete their own servant-hood coupons. For those in Group 1 who have already completed theirs, distribute copies of activity page 12C and let them decode the phrases describing ways Jesus served.

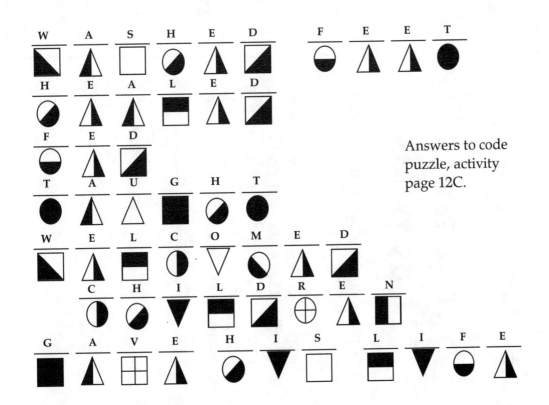

Answers to code puzzle, activity page 12C.

# Servanthood Coupons

Read the Scriptures and supply the missing words. Then fill out the servanthood coupons with the names of people you will serve, and the tasks you will do to serve them. Remember to sign the coupons, cut them apart, and present them to the people for whom you made them.

**SERVANTHOOD COUPON**

In Galatians 5:13 Christians are told to _Serve_

each other with _love_

I will show love as I _____
for you.

Presented to _____

Signed _____

**SERVANTHOOD COUPON**

The Bible says to _Love_ the _Lord_

with all your heart (Romans 12:11).

I will _____ with all my heart because I'm serving the Lord too.

Presented to _____

Signed _____

**SERVANTHOOD COUPON**

I learn in 1 Peter 4:11 that the person who

serves should with the _Strength_ that _God gives_

I will _____ for you with the strength that God gives me.

Presented to _____

Signed _____

**SERVANTHOOD COUPON**

Ephesians 6:7 says to work as if you were

the _Servants of God_

I will _____
for you as if I were doing it for Jesus.

Presented to _____

Signed _____

**SERVANTHOOD COUPON**

In Psalm 100:2 I read, "_Worship_ the

_Lord_ with _Gladness_."

I will joyfully _____ for you.

Presented to _____

Signed _____

**SERVANTHOOD COUPON**

Second Corinthians 9:7 says, "God loves a

_Cheerful giver_."

I will cheerfully _____
for you.

Presented to _____

Signed _____

© 1992 by The Standard Publishing Company.
Permission is granted to photocopy this page for ministry purposes only—not for resale.

# A Servant/A King

Check out these Scriptures and fill in the blanks.

**Isaiah 42:1**—God calls Jesus His _____ and says He is _____ with Jesus.

**Acts 3:13**—God gives _____ to Jesus, who is _____ _____.

**Matthew 20:28**—Jesus did not come _____, but Jesus came to

_____ others.

**Luke 22:27**—Jesus said He is like a _____.

**Philippians 2:7**—Jesus made himself _____, taking the _____ of a

_____. He became _____.

### Compose a prayer.

1. Write a sentence telling who God is and who we are.

   God, You are the _____ and we are your

   servants.

2. Write a sentence praising God for making a plan to

   save us.

3. Write a sentence praising Jesus for becoming a

   servant to us.

4. Write a sentence describing ways that Jesus served

   us.

5. Write a sentence describing your feelings.

   When I think of how You have served us, I feel

   _____.

6. Write a sentence of commitment, telling God that you want to serve Him.

7. Write a sentence describing one way you will serve Him.

© 1992 by The Standard Publishing Company.
Permission is granted to photocopy this page for ministry purposes only—not for resale.

# Ways Jesus Served Others

Decode the phrases below to discover ways Jesus served others.

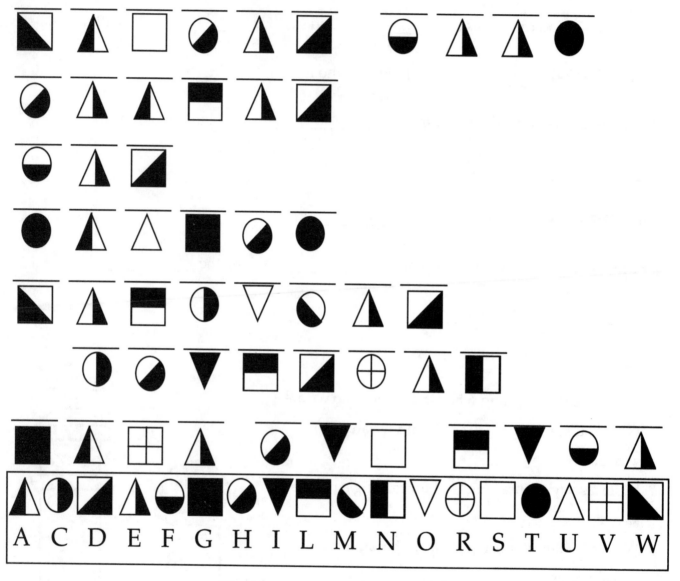

How can you serve these people?

little children

elderly people

parents

neighbors

brothers and sisters

church

poor people/people with special needs

© 1992 by The Standard Publishing Company.
Permission is granted to photocopy this page for ministry purposes only—not for resale.

# Wholehearted Obedience

## Worship Focus

Worship God because He commands wholehearted obedience.

## Transition Time

(10-15 minutes)

Bring ingredients for three batches of cookies and a toaster oven, or make arrangements to use the oven in the church kitchen. Divide pupils into three groups and give each group a copy of the recipe and the ingredients for one batch. Make these variations in the copies of the recipes you give them:

Batch 1, leave out an ingredient
Batch 2, bake slightly too long
Batch 3, bake according to the recipe.

When groups have prepared and baked their cookies, show a poster-sized copy of the correct recipe.

If baking won't fit into your class situation, have groups prepare a drink mix. Have one group leave out sugar or add salt instead, and another add too much water.

## Launching the Theme

(10 minutes)

How many kinds of obedience can you name? Think about this for a moment. If you can't imagine any, remember the parable of the two sons: the one said he would obey his father, but didn't. The other said he wouldn't obey his father, but later changed his mind. Those would be two examples of different kinds of obedience. What is the outcome or result for these? Let's compare them to following a recipe. When we obey only some of God's commands, it is like leaving out an ingredient. When we follow His commands, but not exactly, as when the cookies baked just a few minutes too long, the end result is not what was intended. What does this teach us about the importance of obeying? During today's session we will explore the difference between obeying God wholeheartedly and obeying Him just enough to get by. We'll see what Jesus thought about obedience. We'll find out what happened to some who totally ignored God's commands. And we'll discover God's attitude toward people who realize their mistakes and change their minds about the kind of obedience they want to give God.

# Building the Theme

●●●●●●●●●●●●●●●●●●●
(30 minutes)

**1. Scripture.** Pupils will examine Scriptures and prepare a chart displaying different degrees of obedience. Provide Bibles, a large sheet of newsprint, and markers. **What is the difference between inward obedience and outward obedience?** Let pupils respond. Conclude that outward is surface level, the appearance of obedience, but perhaps only temporary in nature. **In today's parable abut the two sons (Matthew 12), which son showed outward obedience and which showed inward? The labels get mixed up as the parable proceeds, don't they? The son who first said yes failed to follow through. So we would label his outward. The son who first said no then changed his mind and obeyed, so we would label his inward obedience.**

**The Pharisees (religious leaders in Jesus' time) are a great example of the outward obedience. They did everything to look good on the outside, but they allowed their hearts to become proud and mean and greedy on the inside. The Bible tells us how Jesus described them. Let's read to find out.** Have pupils look up these verses and discover what Jesus called the Pharisees.

Matthew 23:16—blind guides
Matthew 23:33—snakes and vipers
Matthew 23:27—whitewashed tombs

Have pupils prepare a brief charade to portray these so that the rest of the group can guess.

Provide a sheet of newsprint and markers. **Now let's dig a little deeper and pinpoint the exact actions that Jesus condemned. We're looking for three difference levels of obedience. Each level relates to a part of the body.** Have pupils find the verses and discover the kind of obedience mentioned. Then have them draw an outline of a human body on the newsprint, and write in the kind of obedience next to the corresponding body part. Ask, **What would be a modern example of each of these levels of obedience?** If you wish, have students add pictures of the Pharisees as Jesus described them. Prepare to explain the chart during the large group time.

lip level obedience—Isaiah 29:13, Ezekiel 33:31
eye level obedience—Colossians 3:22
heart level obedience—Joel 2:12, 13

**2. Scripture.** Pupils will read about Bible people who disobeyed God, and discover the consequences of disobedience. Provide copies of activity page 13A, Bibles, and pencils or pens.

## The Price You Pay

Read the Scriptures. Discover how the person disobeyed God and what consequences he suffered.

| Scripture | Bible Person | Disobeyed God by... | Consequence of Disobedience |
|---|---|---|---|
| Judges 15:17-21 | Samson | | |
| 1 Samuel 13:8-14 | Saul | | |
| Numbers 20:8-12 | Moses | | |
| Genesis 3:6,23 | Eve and Adam | | |
| 1 Kings 11:9-13 | Solomon | | |

Complete the postcard below by writing a message from one of the Bible characters above. Give advice to a person who is considering disobeying God.

POST CARD

TO: _____

Have each pupil select one Scripture, read it, and jot down how the Bible person disobeyed and the consequence. Have pupils share with each other what they learn. Then have them write a postcard as if the Bible person is sending a message of advice and warning to someone who is considering disobeying.

During *Sharing in Worship*, this group will present their chart to the large group.

To do so, they will need to copy the chart on a chalkboard, marker board, overhead transparency, or large sheet of paper. Provide supplies you have available.

For a sample of the completed chart, see the last page of this session.

**3. Devotion.** Pupils will give advice to characters with commitment problems. Have students locate and read the Scriptures below. Then have them discuss the situation and choose a Scripture verse as the basis of their advice to help the person overcome his problem.

Here are the situations:

1. Mike is a complainer. He usually does his chores, but all the time he is complaining about how unfair his parents are, or how easy his younger brother has it, or how no one understands him.

2. Terry is a half-hearted worker. She does the parts of the job that are easy, and slacks off on the rest. She acts as though she doesn't know how to finish, or says she has hurt herself or gets a headache. She drags along in a pouty sort of way, hoping her mom will get fed up with her and tell her to quit.

3. Ben carries out his responsibilities only if he feels like it. "I'm a little tired today. I don't think I'll get up for church."

4. Candy is a quitter. She says she will do something and starts to do it, but she doesn't keep her commitment. She said she would water her neighbors' garden while they were gone. She did it only for the first few days, and then forgot until the day before they came. She said she would baby-sit, but when her friends wanted her to go to a movie with them, she canceled at the last minute.

Here are the Scripture verses:

Galatians 6:9—"Let us not become weary in doing good."

Colossians 3:23—"Whatever you do, work at it with all your heart, as working for the Lord."

1 Corinthians 15:58—"Stand firm. Let nothing move you. Always give

yourselves fully to the work of the Lord."

Titus 3:14—"Our people must learn to devote themselves to doing what is good, in order that they may provide for daily necessities and not live unproductive lives."

1 Timothy 4:12—"Don't let anyone look down on you because you are young, but set an example for the believers . . ."

**4. Devotion.** Pupils will study Scriptures about repentance and complete a chart comparing godly and worldly repentance. **Let's imagine two small children are fighting. Their mom steps in to settle the matter. She finds out who started the fight, or who hit whom first. Then she tells the culprit, "What do you say?" The culprit hangs his head and mutters, "Sorry," but not very convincingly. Then the mom says, "Say it like you mean it." That scene is something we may have been a part of. The Bible identifies two ways to be sorry for wrongs. One of them is not very convincing. Let's find 2 Corinthians 7:10 and see how these are described.** Distribute activity page 13B. Have students explain the diagram of 2 Corinthians 7:10.

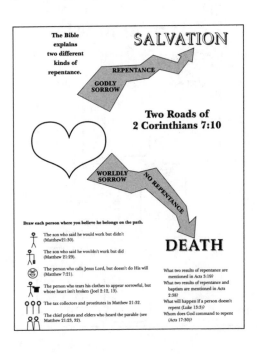

The Bible explains two different kinds of repentance.

SALVATION

REPENTANCE

GODLY SORROW

Two Roads of 2 Corinthians 7:10

WORLDLY SORROW

NO REPENTANCE

DEATH

Draw each person where you believe he belongs on the path.

The son who said he would work but didn't (Matthew 21:30).

The son who said he wouldn't work but did (Matthew 21:29).

The person who calls Jesus Lord, but doesn't do His will (Matthew 7:21).

The person who tears his clothes to appear sorrowful, but whose heart isn't broken (Joel 2:12, 13).

The tax collectors and prostitutes in Matthew 21:32.

The chief priests and elders who heard the parable (see Matthew 21:23, 32).

What two results of repentance are mentioned in Acts 3:19?

What two results of repentance and baptism are mentioned in Acts 2:38?

What will happen if a person doesn't repent (Luke 13:3)?

Whom does God command to repent (Acts 17:30)?

Discuss where on the diagram you would place the characters listed. Then have them find the verses and answer the other questions about repentance.

1. What two results of repentance are mentioned in Acts 3:19? (sins wiped out, times of refreshing come)
2. What two results of repentance and baptism are mentioned in Acts 2:38? (sins forgiven, gift of Holy Spirit)
3. What will happen if a person doesn't repent? See Luke 13:3 (he will perish).
4. Who does God command to repent? See Acts 17:30 (all people everywhere).

Ask for a volunteer to show and summarize the chart during *Sharing in Worship.*

**5. Personal Praise.** Pupils will prepare "road signs" giving biblical directions. Provide copies of activity page 13C, *New International* or *King James* Bibles, pencils, poster board, and markers. Maybe you've heard before that the word *repent* means to change your mind or to turn around. Today we're going to look at some specific ways the Bible tells us to turn. Then we'll summarize that advice on posters that look like road signs, indicating a turn in the road. Have pupils complete the activity page, then decide who will make larger copies of each of the road signs to display and explain during *Sharing in Worship.*

1 Peter 3:11—turn from evil and do good
1 Timothy 6:20—turn away from godless chatter
Proverbs 2:2—turn your ear to wisdom
Acts 3:19—turn to God
Ezekiel 33:11—turn from your evil ways
Acts 26:18—turn from darkness to light
Psalm 119:36—turn my heart toward your statutes and not toward selfish gain.
Psalm 119:37—turn my eyes away from worthless things

**6. Prayer.** Pupils will prepare a prayer of commitment based on selected Scripture verses. Provide scratch paper, Bibles, a sheet of newsprint, pens, scissors, and a supply of red or pink construction paper. Give each pupil one or two of the Scripture references printed below. Key phrases are given for your reference only. Then have the pupils discuss the verses and decide how they'll order the verses to comprise their prayer. Have pupils write out the prayer on the sheet of newsprint, and decide which group member or members will read the prayer during *Sharing in Worship.*

Next, have the pupils cut out hearts from the construction paper, about four to a sheet. Make enough to distribute one heart to each person during *Sharing in Worship.* Then have pupils copy one of the other Bible verses on each of the hearts.

Use these verses to compose the prayer:

Psalm 119:10—I seek you with all my heart.

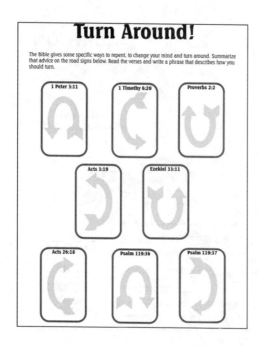

**Turn Around!**

The Bible gives some specific ways to repent, to change your mind and turn around. Summarize that advice on the road signs below. Read the verses and write a phrase that describes how you should turn.

1 Peter 3:11     1 Timothy 6:20     Proverbs 2:2

Acts 3:19     Ezekiel 33:11

Acts 26:18     Psalm 119:36     Psalm 119:37

Psalm 119:34—Give me understanding and I will keep your law and obey it with all my heart

Psalm 86:11—Teach me your way, O Lord; give me an undivided heart

Psalm 86:12—I will praise you with all my heart

Use these verses on the construction paper hearts:

Deuteronomy 6:5—Love the Lord with all your heart

Psalm 119:2—Blessed are they who seek him with all their heart

Proverbs 3:5—Trust in the Lord with all your heart

Jeremiah 29:13—You will seek me and find me when you see me with all your heart

# Sharing in Worship
●●●●●●●●●●●●●●●●●●
## (20-25 minutes)

Omit any section if you did not offer the corresponding activity.

**Call to Worship:** Have a pupil or assistant read Isaiah 55:6, 7.

**Music:** Sing "I'm Your Lord," "I Have Decided to Follow Jesus," or other songs dealing with wholehearted devotion to God.

**Scripture** (Groups 1 and 2): **We began today by talking about different kinds of obedience. Remember how we applied the idea of complete obedience to following a cookie recipe? We talked about inward obedience and outward obedience. The Pharisees (religious leaders of Jesus' time) are a great example of outward obedience. They did everything to look good on the outside, but they allowed their hearts to become proud and mean and greedy.**

**Jesus had some descriptive names for the Pharisees. Group 1 will help us to discover them now.** Group 1 presents their charades. Then follow up by saying, **Group 1 dug a little deeper into this subject. They will show us a few more degrees of obedience.** Group 1 presents their chart.

**The Bible warns us about what happens when we choose to disobey. Group 2 studied some Bible characters whose lives are good examples of what not to do.** Have Group 2 show their chart and read the postcards they wrote.

**Devotion** (Group 3): **You might be thinking to yourself, "I know I sometimes fail to obey God totally, but my problems aren't like these Bible people's. I don't offer sacrifices when I'm not supposed to. And I don't eat fruit from a forbidden tree." So let's get practical. Group 3 discussed situations and problems that we might identify with.** Have Group 3 share the situations they discussed and their advice for handling such problems.

**Music:** Sing "Trust and Obey" as a group.

**Devotion** (Group 4): **We've seen that God wants our total obedience. When we look at our lives and admit that we have areas where we could improve our obedience level, we are in the process of "repenting" or changing our minds about our behavior. We are like the second son in the parable who changed his mind and decided to go work for his father. But guess what? Just as there are different kinds of obedience, there are also different kinds of repentance. Group 4 has an explanation of this.** Have a member or members of Group 4 show and explain their "road map."

**Lord's Supper:** All of us are a little like the son who said he would go work for the father and then didn't go. We all have days or times when it is hard to obey God. We end the day or week regretting some action or realizing

| Scripture | Bible Person | Disobeyed God by . . . | Consequences of Disobedience |
|---|---|---|---|
| Judges 15:17-21 | Samson | broke Nazarite vow | blinded and imprisoned |
| 1 Samuel 13:8-14 | Saul | sacrificed without Samuel | God took kingdom, gave to David |
| Numbers 20:8-12 | Moses | struck rock instead of speaking to it | couldn't enter Promised Land |
| Genesis 3:6, 23 | Adam and Eve | ate from tree | banished from Garden of Eden |
| 1 Kings 11:9-13 | Solomon | followed other gods | God divided kingdom |

Answers to *The Price You Pay* chart, activity page 13A.

we've slipped away from God's plan.

The Lord's Supper is like a signpost that points the way back to God. We are reminded who we are—friends of God whom He has invited to a special meal—and how we got that way—through Jesus' blood, not our own good deeds. The Lord's Supper is a way of reminding us that we are never too far away from God to come back home. The table is always ready. God is always calling us back to Him and helping us to turn to Him. Isaiah 30:15 says, "In repentance and rest is your salvation." Turn back to God and rest peacefully, knowing that He wants you here.

**Personal Praise** (Group 5 and 6): So now you may be thinking that you do indeed want to commit yourself to a higher level of obedience, to turn around your thinking and your actions. Where do you go from here? The Bible never points out a problem without offering a solution. Group 5 made a collection of different instructions about "turning around." Let's see what directions they have for us. Have Group 5 display and explain their road signs.

Now is a time of evaluation and decision. (Have Group 6 distribute the hearts, one to each person, with a pencil.) Use this quiet time to jot down some instructions to yourself. What changes do you want to make in your obedience level? What kind of repentance do you want to take place in your life? What kind of turning away from something do you need to do? Repenting might result in apologizing to someone, forgiving someone, getting rid of something that would be contrary to a new lifestyle, praying, confessing sin, being baptized, beginning a regular Bible study, quitting some bad habit. Allow several moments of quiet time.

**Music:** Use the song "Into My Heart" as a song of commitment for the group.

**Prayer:** Have a member or members of Group 6 read the prayer the small group prepared.

# Closing Moments

• • • • • • • • • • • • • •

## (10-15 minutes)

Play "Whole Heart." Make several large paper hearts from red construction paper. Cut each of the hearts into three or more random-shaped pieces. Have a glue stick, marker, and sheet of paper large enough to mount the heart on for each heart you make.

To play, distribute one random-shaped piece to each pupil. At a signal, the pupils must locate others whose pieces fit with theirs to form a heart. The first group to assemble their heart, use a glue stick to attach it to the sheet of paper, and print on the paper, "Love God and serve Him with your whole heart" wins.

# The Price You Pay

Read the Scriptures. Discover how the person disobeyed God and what consequences he suffered.

| Scripture | Bible Person | Disobeyed God by... | Consequence of Disobedience |
|---|---|---|---|
| Judges 15:17-21 | Samson | | |
| 1 Samuel 13:8-14 | Saul | | |
| Numbers 20:8-12 | Moses | | |
| Genesis 3:6,23 | Eve and Adam | | |
| 1 Kings11:9-13 | Solomon | | |

Complete the postcard below by writing a message from one of the Bible characters above. Give advice to a person who is considering disobeying God.

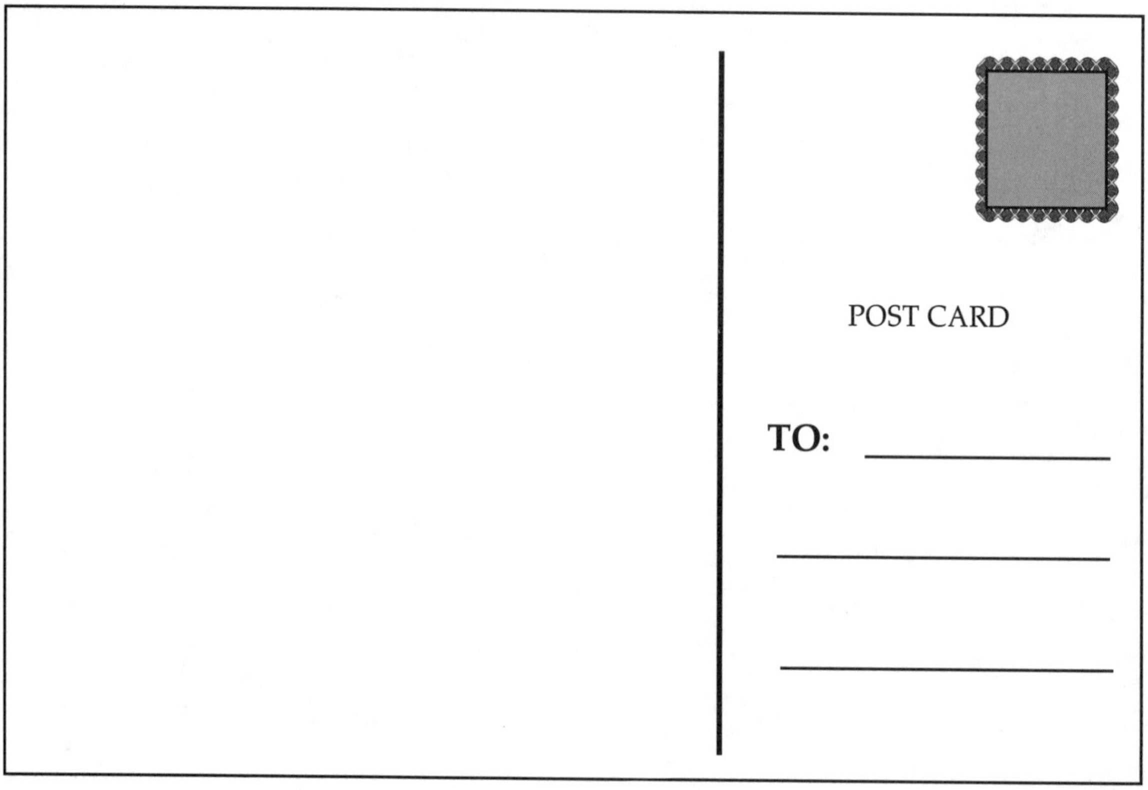

POST CARD

TO: _____

_____

_____

© 1992 by The Standard Publishing Company.
Permission is granted to photocopy this page for ministry purposes only—not for resale.

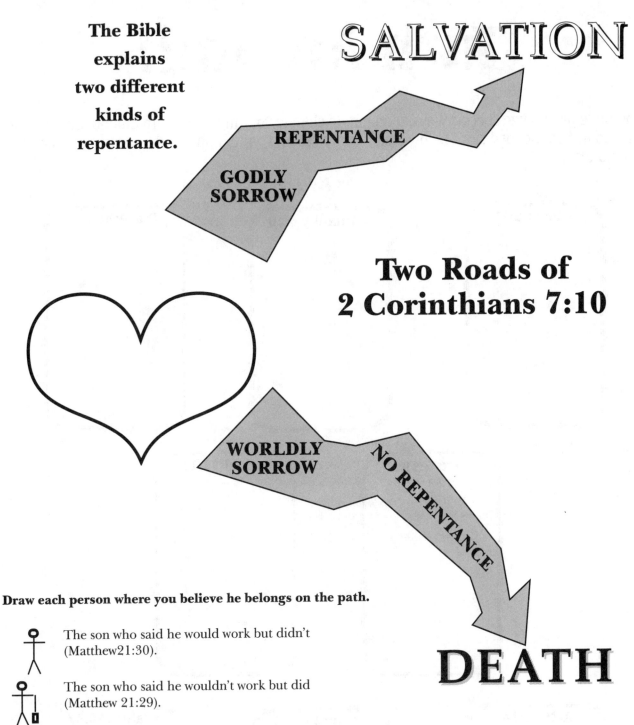

The Bible explains two different kinds of repentance.

SALVATION

REPENTANCE

GODLY SORROW

Two Roads of 2 Corinthians 7:10

WORLDLY SORROW

NO REPENTANCE

DEATH

**Draw each person where you believe he belongs on the path.**

 The son who said he would work but didn't (Matthew 21:30).

The son who said he wouldn't work but did (Matthew 21:29).

The person who calls Jesus Lord, but doesn't do His will (Matthew 7:21).

 The person who tears his clothes to appear sorrowful, but whose heart isn't broken (Joel 2:12, 13).

 The tax collectors and prostitutes in Matthew 21:32.

 The chief priests and elders who heard the parable (see Matthew 21:23, 32).

What two results of repentance are mentioned in Acts 3:19?

What two results of repentance and baptism are mentioned in Acts 2:38?

What will happen if a person doesn't repent (Luke 13:3)?

Whom does God command to repent (Acts 17:30)?

© 1992 by The Standard Publishing Company.
Permission is granted to photocopy this page for ministry purposes only—not for resale.

# Turn Around!

The Bible gives some specific ways to repent, to change your mind and turn around. Summarize that advice on the road signs below. Read the verses and write a phrase that describes how you should turn.

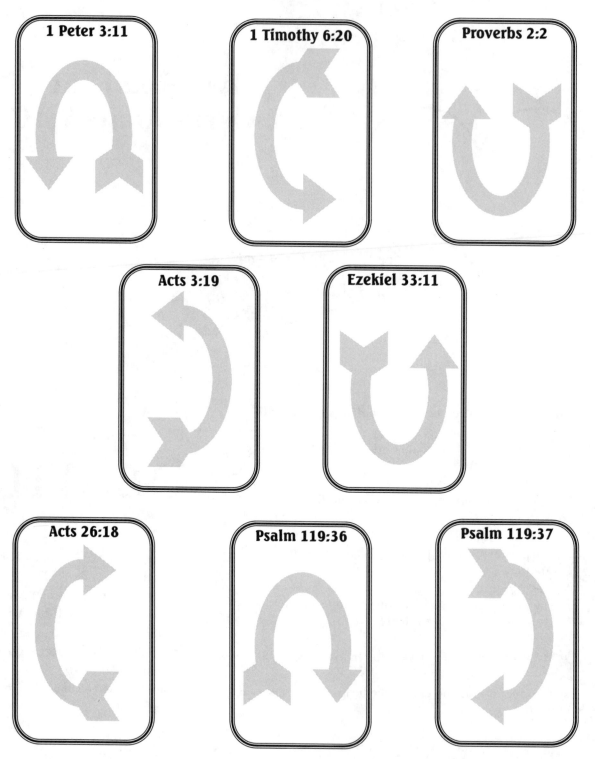

© 1992 by The Standard Publishing Company.
Permission is granted to photocopy this page for ministry purposes only—not for resale.